M000033297

Married For Good

Married For Good

R. Paul Stevens

REGENT COLLEGE PUBLISHING
VANCOUVER, BRITISH COLUMBIA

MARRIED FOR GOOD
Copyright © 1986 by R. Paul Stevens

First published in 1986 by Inter-Varsity Christian Fellowship
of the United States of America
    (ISBN 0-87784-603-0)

This edition reproduced 1997 by Regent College Publishing,
an imprint of the Regent College Bookstore,
5800 University Boulevard, Vancouver, B.C. V6T 2E4

Printed in Canada

All rights reserved. No part of this publication may be reproduced, stored in a re-
trieval system, or transmitted, in any form or by any means, electronic, mechani-
cal, photocopying, recording of otherwise, without the prior written permission of
the publisher, except in the case of brief quotations embodied in critical articles
and reviews.

Unless otherwise noted, all Scripture quotations are from the Holy Bible: *New International Version* (NIV), copyright © 1978 by the New York International Bible
Society and used by permission.

Library of Congress Cataloging-in-Publication Data

Stevens, R. Paul, 1937-
   Married for good.

   Bibliography: p.

   1. Marriage—Religious aspects—Christianity.
I. Title.

BV835.S875 1997

ISBN 1-57383-087-9

Gail, my covenant partner

Acknowledgments

*Thanks to the following
people for reading
the manuscript and
helping constructively:
Dr. Peter Davids,
Paddy Ducklow, Carol
Anderson, Andrew
Le Peau and Mickey
Maudlin. Special thanks
to Joan Lloyd Guest,
the editor who shepherded
this book out of a
fledgling idea many
months ago.*

Foreword

Within the space of a generation, a strange and disturbing thing has happened. We have passed from a time where one traditionally spoke of marrying and raising a family as life's high priority and *then* finding a job in order to make that priority a possibility. Now we live in a day where one speaks of pursuing a career as the issue of central importance and making room, if possible, for a family . . . afterward.

The price of this shift is exorbitant. The day is in sight when half of the entering college population will come from single-parent families. Increasingly, people in relationships lack the appropriate models of fidelity and servanthood, and thus fear that they too will fail in their commitments. I am struck with the sense of brokenness that permeates this generation. "My mother and father have a more active date life than I do," one woman says of her separated parents. Another observes, "I don't think I've ever seen a marriage that I thought was attractive."

Now we find ourselves in a time when a new generation may have to go back to "square one" and learn the rudiments of enduring relationships all over again. That is why Paul Stevens provides us with such a significant contribution in this book, *Married for Good*.

Stevens has indeed gone back to square one and taken us to the roots of the biblical teaching on relationships. This is not a "how-to" book, although one will gather many ideas about how to. It is a "what-does-it-mean?" book and a "why-are-these-things-important?" book. After reading it you will understand all over again that those who follow the Lord are prom-ise-makers, ones who establish covenants and then commit to keeping them. This covenant-making and keeping, I believe, is the highest task of a human being.

Two people committing themselves to a covenant that is unique, total, indissoluble and sacred is, Paul Stevens con-cludes, awesome—especially when we remember that we live in a world that thinks relationships are expendable whenever personal convenience or pleasure is no longer served. But I believe with Paul Stevens that it is also extraordinary because a vow taken is heard in heaven and honored by the living God.

This is not a simplistic treatment of Christian marriage. No easy answers here. But what the reader is going to find is a challenge, a call to the adventure of commitment between two human beings.

We have arrived at a time where there is room for a relational revolution, the moment where a new generation of Christians can reveal the unique and powerful love of Christ as they commit themselves to one another. Possible? By all means. And Paul Stevens has provided a textbook that will make it happen.

I am delighted to commend *Married for Good* to you. It sets a high standard and extends an invitation to a high adventure.

Gordon MacDonald
April 1986

How to Read This Book for All It's Worth

On Your Own
Like any other book on marriage this book can be read for personal pleasure and benefit. One important difference is that there are exercises at the end of every chapter to help you make your own learning discoveries. If you are already married, these studies may help you *make changes in yourself,* rather than to make demands on your spouse.

As an Engaged Couple
Those not-yet-married will find many useful exercises to increase marriage readiness. The book is full of good things to talk about *before* you get married. Take a chapter each week, read the material separately and do the exercises together.

As a Married Couple
Many couples wish to deepen their marriage relationship but don't know how. Here is a tool for couples to work *together* on marriage enrichment. It will be most profitable when used on a weekly basis by setting aside one evening a week as "your night." By reading the chapter beforehand and doing the exercises together, I think you will find the time rewarding, stimulating and, hopefully, fun. Some couples could plan a personal retreat—perhaps in a local hotel—and combine the leisure of this special time with guided discovery learning.

In a Couples Study Group
Not only local churches but groups of neighbors are increas-

ingly finding the value of meeting in groups of six to twelve for a period of time for the purpose of enriching their marriages. This text offers a guide and exercise book which each couple in the group should have. The leader of the group should read in advance of the first meeting a copy of *Married for Good*. An important discipline to be accepted by the group is to agree *not to talk about their children with their spouses or with other couples during the meetings*. Many couples have become child-centered and to have a time to focus on their own relationship is very healthy. It is also the emphasis in the Bible. First we are husband and wife, then parents.

In a Marriage Enrichment Weekend
A weekend away from the kids, a special romantic setting and a nonthreatening environment are the ingredients of a big step forward for many couples wanting to improve their marriages. Most churches now try to plan such weekends from time to time to prevent marriage breakdown. It is more strategic to prevent breakdown than to cure an already sick marriage. But it is difficult to find experienced and mature leaders to guide such weekends.

By using this book a local church *can conduct its own weekend*. My wife and I have been leading such weekends for fifteen years and many of the exercises in this guide are the fruit of our experience. The great advantage of conducting your own marriage enrichment weekend—as compared with attending nationally advertised seminars—is that you can continue to care for and nurture the couples you are with long after the weekend is over. Further, the process of preparing for the weekends and conducting it is an important equipping tool for developing ministry among all the members of the local church.

Part One:
Laying the Foundation

1
First Things First

MY FAVORITE PLACE ON EARTH, after home, is a small rustic cabin on an island off the Pacific coastline. Although only thirty miles from home, it might as well be another world, a world without telephones and date books. And it is there that I learned the hardest and most important lesson about marriage: the need for an adequate foundation.

We had scraped together a few dollars to buy a lot by the sea. I hadn't intended to build a cabin but thought that a "cabin tent" on a twelve-foot-square platform would work fine for the family.

The ground was sloping and rocky right down to where the salt water lapped against the shore, not an easy place to build.

So I created a simple tent platform from two-by-sixes and put it on four posts braced on boulders appropriate for the sloping land. This would be secure enough, I thought.

I soon discovered that the cost of a cabin-tent large enough for my family was astronomical. For the same price I could buy all the materials needed for a twelve-by-twelve *wooden* cabin. My plans and vision grew. I began to install the panels of a prefabricated cedar cabin on the tent platform.

It was beautiful, that lovely shed-roofed cabin snuggled in a cluster of arbutus trees under towering Douglas firs. I had constructed the cabin well, erecting twelve panels on the platform, installing and bolting the roof rafters, laying down plywood underlay on the roof and waterproofing it with tarpaper.

But I had forgotten the foundation. I remember looking rather anxiously at the sag developing in the cross beams supporting the weight of the cabin. One of the posts, a creosote-impregnated log salvaged from the sea, was beginning to tilt forward in sympathy with the slope of the land.

That first summer we offered our "resort" to some friends who love the out-of-doors as we do. John was handy with his hands, and so I asked him to keep an eye on the foundation. A few weeks later, when I rounded the point in our small sailboat, I sighed in relief to see the cabin still standing. John had raised the sagging beams with a car jack and propped up one place with a beach-combed post. But I knew that, before I could do anything else on the cabin, I had to do what should have been done at the beginning.

The Basis of Marriage

I had not built a foundation. Just so, some people find themselves in a deepening relationship with a friend that they never intended to marry. They fail to lay the foundation for a *lasting* relationship. They continue to build the structure while ignoring what they need most—the covenant, the foundation. It's not easy to build a foundation when the cabin is already in place. It is better to build the foundation *first*. But it's also better to build "after the fact" rather than never, if you have something that looks like a house.

Many who read this book will already be married. My central message is that real marriage is founded on an unconditional covenant to belong together for life. You may discover that you have a nice cabin built on a weak platform. But it is better to build the needed foundation now, as awkward as that task may be, than assume it's too late.

Others will come to a book on covenant marriage as engaged or about-to-be engaged couples. In that case I pray that this book will help you build a real and a lasting marriage.

And some may read this who will not yet have an intended bride or groom but will sense that, in God's sovereignty, they may eventually marry. To be a marriageable person is more important than to be married. The qualities that make for a good covenant marriage are the same qualities we should all develop if we want to be fully human and to truly follow the most fully human and divine person—Jesus. If ever there was a marriageable person who chose to be single, it was Jesus. He showed us that our God and Father loves to dwell with us in *covenant*. And, married or not, we should desire *the capacity* to make, keep and fill a marriage covenant.

What is missing in most marriages today is what the Bible identifies as the heart of marriage: a covenant. Everything else is superstructure. Understanding expectations, developing good communication (especially sexual), gaining skills in conflict resolution, discovering appropriate roles or creating new ones, making our marriages fun and free, becoming spiritual friends and sharing a ministry—these are the walls, the roof, the wiring, the plumbing and the heating. They are essential

foundation is so important.

to the whole. But if there is no foundation, they will collapse with the whole building.

Covenant Marriage

My daughter was telling us at supper one night what her psychology professor had to say about getting married.

"First," he had said, "don't marry until you can be sure that when (not if) you get out of it you will have your own money, your own assets, your own profession and your own circle of friends. That will reduce the hurt.

"Second, the purpose of marriage is to be happy.

"And third, remember that the happiest day for a married couple is the wedding day. They will feel closer then than at any future time. In all probability children will push them farther apart. From the wedding day on it is a downhill run."

What is so destructive in our society is not the undermining of individual marriages but the destruction of the very *idea* of marriage. This professor knew nothing of marriage as an indissoluble covenant. Covenant marriage as presented in this book is *a lifelong covenant partnership, solemnly made before God, in which a man and a woman agree to belong together as long as they both shall live.*

It is one thing to show truth and compassion to those who have felt the hurt of marriage failure and have gone through divorce. Many have suffered the secret pain of sexual abuse, physical violence and alcoholism and then, when they divorced, have been further hurt by the rejection they receive from the Christian community. Probably no one ever gets over a divorce, and Christians in particular should demonstrate non-judgmental love. But it is quite a different matter to approve the *idea* of divorce as a normal experience and to stand by silently as marriage is violated and the covenant eroded.

A Contract for Happiness? Studies on marital happiness confirm what the professor said: many marriages peak on the honeymoon. In other words, that is when they reach their highest point of contentment—*if evaluated by the gauge of our culture*. But are these feelings of personal warmth and fulfillment the Maker's design and the Maker's goals for marriage?

A chart of an "average" couple's marital journey may look radically different when gauged by the covenant. Imagine a graph, not of the decline of marital satisfaction or happiness, but of the growth of covenant qualities in partners over the years of marriage. "Covenant satisfaction" might be a good term to describe the fruits of covenant making: increased faithfulness, character development, troth, comfort in the relationship and love. But these are the fruit of a covenant rather than its cause. The important question in marriage is not so much "Do you love me?" as "Will you love me, and will you love me no matter what?"

Of course we all wish for happiness and feelings of love in our marriages. But our greatest need is for growth in Christlikeness. Covenant marriage promises us what we *need*—and often gives what we *want* as a spin-off.

In the covenant we should expect to grow more mature. Why not take the fruit of the Spirit (Gal 5:22-23) as the ultimate measure of covenant satisfaction? Should we not anticipate increased kindness, self-control, gentleness and patience in ourselves and in the relationship as the years go by? Isn't that more biblically realistic than wishing to "live happily ever after," or to meet all of each other's emotional needs or to become fulfilled persons?

Grounds for Hope. Books abound to help us fine-tune our abilities to communicate and meet each other's needs. We need these helps. But none of us can keep our marriages permanently fine-tuned. The power will go off sometime. A covenant foundation motivates us to reach out once more and to make a success of a marriage which for the moment seems to be "for worse." The covenant gives us grounds for hope.

A covenant is not a padlock on the relationship. That would make marriage a prison. A covenant is rather an elastic link between two hearts. When they move apart, a tug reminds them they belong. Or, a covenant is a net beneath two trapeze artists. It is risky business, this high-wire stunt, and they will undoubtedly fall sometime. But the safety net beneath them holds. Or imagine two huge hands, palms upward and together, holding a tiny couple. We play out the drama of our marriages, the pas de deux of living, but we do it safely in the hands of a gracious God who is determined to dwell in covenant with us.

Far from being a relational prison, a covenant offers the only true basis and hope for all the other marriage by-products we want—love, sexual satisfaction, personal growth and spiritual friendship. Where there are no roots, the fruits wither all too quickly. P. T. Forsyth, a Congregational theologian writing at the turn of the century, wrote this: "The fixity of marriage is the moral condition for converting the decay of passion into the growth of real affection, especially under Christian culture and power."[1] We need covenant "fixity" to see love grow.

Society and the Covenant

North American society is committing marital suicide today. The most dangerous thing happening is not the breakdown of individual marriages, tragic as that is, but that people are entering marriage with the thought that they can leave it.

Covenant marriage itself, however, is *not* what is failing. In a lifelong covenant, partners agree to belong together not "so long as they both shall love" but "as long as they both shall live." Such a covenant is an affair of society. It must be witnessed by family and friends and acknowledged by the state;

and it is mysteriously indwelt by God.

David Atkinson in *To Have and to Hold* defines covenant as "an agreement between two parties based on promise, which includes these four elements: first, an undertaking of committed faithfulness made by one party to the other (or by each to the other); secondly, the acceptance of that undertaking by the other party; thirdly, public knowledge of such an undertaking and its acceptance; and fourthly, the growth of a personal relationship based on and expressive of such a commitment."[2]

That is the foundation. What point is there in building walls and roof, installing light and power and heat if the foundation is missing? This covenant idea of marriage has not been tried and found wanting. It has been found too difficult, or not convenient and so not tried. Not enough people today are getting married in this complete sense, and many think they are married but are not.

The covenant today is being assaulted. It used to be that when two people got married they assumed they were going to stay married for life. "We meant it for keeps," our parents tell us. But let's face it. All the social forces of their time conspired both to get them married and to keep them married. If they wanted companionship, sexual fulfillment, economic security, children and social acceptance, they had to get married and stay that way. Many of those marriages were empty covenants, but they were covenants nonetheless. They could have been filled.

Today new social forces conspire to break the covenant apart and to reduce marriage to a temporary need-meeting relationship between two people. Now people can get companionship, sexual fulfillment, economic security, children and social acceptance just as easily in the single life or in a living-together arrangement. And sometimes marriage would be a definite disadvantage. "I would no more think of marrying the man I'm living with," said one middle-aged widow, "than fly to the moon! I'd lose two pensions if I did."

Four cultural forces in particular have conspired to undermine the idea of marriage. *Humanism* teaches that marriage is just a personal matter, that no God cares or will hold us to our word. *Relativism* in moral issues makes it easy to set our own rules—and to break them if we change our minds. *Selfism*, the logical child of relativism and humanism, tells us we must reach for our full potential as persons. If you must leave a marriage to find yourself or to actualize yourself, so be it. Fritz Perls put it this way: "I do my thing, and you do your thing. I am not in this world to live up to your expectations, and you are not in this world to live up to mine. And if by some chance we meet, it's beautiful!"[3] The fourth "ism," American *pragmatism*, encourages us to make our decisions totally on the basis of what works best for us, and so if a marriage is not satisfying, then get out.

Herman by Jim Unger © 1983, Universal Press Syndicate. Reprinted with permission. All rights reserved.

Psychoanalyst R. D. Laing describes the current state of affairs by observing how "the official dates of public events can be out of phase with the structure of experience."[4] He uses Jack and Jill as a prototype for a typical case:

Jack and Jill were married in 1960. There were over 100 wedding guests. Nevertheless Jack has never *felt* married to Jill, and Jill only began to feel "really" married to Jack some months after the wedding. Although Jack has never felt married to Jill, he believes he is because he can remember going through a ceremony that he knows is called a "marriage." . . . But Jill is not satisfied. . . . One night she started to say in front of the children that he wasn't a real husband. That she was married to him, but he wasn't married to her.[5]

Many people repeat the traditional vows in a church wedding ceremony thinking that they mean them. And in all probability they do mean them *when they say them.* But when the going gets tough, it is not the vows that the couple remember. What surfaces instead is the fruit of our cultural norms which say, "My personal happiness is what counts." Vows of yesterday are easily forgotten.

While in prison Dietrich Bonhoeffer wrote about this mood as he reflected on how quickly people forgot about a night's bombing.

Does it not explain why we sit so lightly to the ties of love and marriage, or friendship and loyalty? Nothing holds us, nothing is firm. Everything is here today and gone tomorrow. Goodness, beauty and truth, however, and all great accomplishments need time, permanence and memory, or else they deteriorate. The man who has no urge to do his duty to the past and to shape the future is a man without a memory, and there seems to me no way of getting hold of such a person and bringing him to his senses. Every word, even if it impresses him for a moment, goes through one ear and out of the other. What is to be done about him?[6]

Indeed, what *can* we do? Marriage is in danger today, not because forty per cent of North American marriages end in divorce, but because the vows are made with the idea that marriage *could* be terminated.[7]

With an astonishing relevance Forsyth wrote that to dissolve "the great divine Triad of Father, Mother, Child, would require a force equal at least to that which made society itself."[8] Are we facing a force of that intensity in our society? I believe we are. But I am profoundly convinced that the covenant itself is a stronger force than the pressures of disintegration. The recovery of the biblical concept of covenant—the heart of marriage itself—is the urgent task of those of us who believe in God and believe in marriage. It is the covenant that our infinite personal God conspires with us to keep, to bless and to fill.

"Therefore what God has joined together" (Mt 19:6) is not an endorsement of two Christians making a liaison, or two agnostics secretly or publicly united in a common bed in a "trial marriage." Marriage cannot be tried. God joins covenant partners—whether believers or not—when they marry, as an old service phrased it, "as God's Word doth allow." Let us explore this mystery together.

Increasingly my wife, Gail, and I get the opportunity to visit with couples *before* they get engaged. It is the best time to seek counsel as, once engaged, the wedding machine becomes an all-embracing preoccupation. A few couples have had the courage to verbalize the question that others fear to ask: "With so many marriages ending in divorce, do you think that we will become a statistic?" What I tell them is the same thing I want to share with you.

You can make a decision today, once and for all, that will mean for certain that your marriage will not become a statistic! It is no vain hope that I offer when I say this. You can decide right now to enter a marriage covenant in which nothing, literally *nothing*, could make you leave. That can be settled once and for all. Indeed it must. In fact, you are not truly married unless you make a divorceless covenant.

In preparing for marriage two people need to agree in their view of marriage, in their refusal to write into the covenant an "emotional loophole." They need to be mature enough to consent fully and freely to such a life covenant. The other considerations—personal compatability, expectations, agendas for power and control, the complementarity of their career plans—are secondary. Discerning covenant capability and covenant compatability are, in my opinion, the most important tasks in getting ready for or strengthening marriage. They are the most neglected areas, but they are also the most hopeful directions we can take. Those who are now married, whether happily or not, need to be convinced about the covenant. Perhaps they need to be converted to it.

Perhaps every marriage has a season of "for worse," when we wonder if we will make it. With the covenant reaffirmed, the question is not *whether,* but *how?* And the "how" is not a hopeless search for the magic key to marital bliss. It is a joint pilgrimage, with each other and God, to stay together for the purposes of the covenant: to belong, to bless and to be blessed. I have sometimes said to people who were legally married, "Get married! Make the covenant now, even if at the time of your legal marriage you were not emotionally mature enough to consent fully, even if your original intentions were wrong, and even if you are now convinced that marriage was a mistake. The worst mistake now would be to ignore what God intended as the foundation of your relationship: the covenant."

Restoring the meaning of the covenant is crucial in our society. It is central to the Bible's message.

An Exercise

Read Genesis 2:18-25. Focus on the three key phrases of 2:24—*leave, cleave* and *one flesh*—by responding to the following questions:

1. What do you think it means to "leave father and mother"? Since this is the public part of the covenant, how is this more than merely physically leaving home?

2. The Hebrew word for "leave" means to forsake. It is the same word used in Psalm 27:10 about abandoning a child. What did you forsake to become married?

3. Is there anything that must still be forsaken for your marriage to have an exclusive basis?

4. What do you think it means to "cleave" to your spouse?

5. How is your friendship with your spouse unlike any other relationship you have?

6. What do you think it means to become "one flesh"?

7. What does the unashamed nakedness (Gen 2:25) suggest about Adam and Eve's relationship?

8. Why would such intimacy be inappropriate with anyone other than one marital partner?

9. Reflecting on God's covenant design in Genesis 2, why can't two become two again after they have become one?

2
God's Covenant Design

IT IS RISKY TO MAKE A LIFELONG covenant. Reflecting on the unique way human beings make a covenant, Lewis Smedes in *Mere Morality* says, "Perhaps the greatest mystery of our humanness is the power to make and keep a vow. For in a vow you freely give yourself over to a permanent identity in the face of an unpredictable future. You will change, the person to whom you make the vow will change, your circumstances will change."[1] This kind of commitment is scary. We need to know what we are getting ourselves into. And that is why we must look carefully at God's expectations before committing ourselves. Those already married and caught in the tension between a culture which stresses self-fulfillment and an unfulfilling phase in their marriage can gain from Scripture a vision for more than "hanging on." A covenant provides the rationale for a married lifestyle that expects to be continuously renewed. More importantly, it takes us to the heart of the Bible's message.

The Marriage of God and His People

The story of God's gracious dealings with his people, both Israel and Israel-in-Christ, is best understood as a marriage covenant between God and his people.[2]

Old Testament scholar R. K. Harrison says that "the Hebrews were unique in the ancient world for their attempts to interpret the whole of their national existence in terms of a solemn covenantal agreement with a single deity."[3] The Jewish novelist Chaim Potok calls the Jews that "covenanted rabble."[4] They were the chosen people. To a nameless group of homeless waifs God said, "I take you. You can make your home with me." And in due course, when they understood that God had redeemed them from Egypt and made them his treasured possession (Ex 19:5), they were able to respond with the other half of the covenant formula: "We take you to be our God." The essence of the covenant is contained in the two-pronged formula, "You will be my people and I will be your God" (Jer 30:22; see also Ex 19:8; Deut 10:12-22).

They are a marriage pair. Each is unique to the other. The people give God a covenant response—"We will have no other gods before you"—because God has already said, "I have no other people before you." And God, in the most radical imagery of the Old Testament, describes himself as a heavenly husband (Is 54:5). The word *covenant* includes the idea of contract or treaty. The Old Testament uses it in referring to a pact, alliance or contract between nations in which each party agrees to do something for the other.[5] Joshua 9:6-15 tells of such a pact between Joshua and the Gibeonites, a contract so binding

that when Saul failed to maintain this sworn covenant obligation, his family was punished (2 Sam 21).

The Hebrew word for covenant, *berith*, is also used for the
constitution or agreement between the monarch and the people (2 Sam 3:21; 5:3; 1 Chron 11:3). It provided what amounted to a limited constitutional monarchy, making Israel unique
in the ancient world.[6] The friendship between David and Jonathan is the only definite mention in the Old Testament of a
covenant between two specific individuals (1 Sam 18:3; 20:8;
23:18). But the *idea* of the covenant as primarily a relationship
runs through the whole Old Testament, particularly when the
word for covenant is used in relation to marriage (Prov 2:17;
Mal 2:14).

The word *testament* is the same as the word *covenant.* The
Christian era confronts us with a double revelation: the New
Covenant (Testament) introduces us to Jesus, and Jesus introduces us to the new covenant. He invites anyone, Jew or non-
Jew, to a marriage with himself in which there will be no
divorce and where there will be much blessing *where we obey
his Word.*

Not only did Jesus endorse human marriage by his presence
and miracle at the wedding in Cana, but he deliberately presented the idea of the kingdom of God, God's glorious rule,
as a wedding feast (Mt 22:1-14). John the Baptist is the friend
of the bridegroom (Jn 3:29). Jesus is the bridegroom (Mt 25:5),
and the church is Christ's bride (Eph 5:25). While in this life
we are technically only engaged or betrothed to Christ (2 Cor
11:2); we look forward to complete union with him and partner-
nership through eternity; at the end of history we will experience the full consummation of his glorious appearing. That
great day, toward which history groans and yearns, must be
understood, John tells us in his vision, as the "marriage supper
of the lamb" (Rev 19:9). Covenant takes us to the heart of what

God has done, is doing and will do. It is a clue to his own heart. Therefore it is a clue to what it means for us humans, made in his image, to live for his glory.

With deep insight the theologian Karl Barth expounds covenant fidelity as "the inner meaning and purpose of our creation as human beings in the divine image."[7] Everything else in creation is simply the framework that enables us to keep the covenant.

The Divine Pattern

Human marriages thus have a divine pattern. They are meant to be *like* God's covenant—in purpose, in permanence, in creativity, in totality. The marriage vows typify the astonishing commitment of God. "I take you," God says in Christ to us. We, as willing covenant partners, are free to consent by responding if we so choose: "We take you." Our salvation is nuptial. To be redeemed in Christ comes from saying "I do" to Christ's marriage proposal. That is the romance of the Bible. God's covenant love is a love "that will not let me go."

The marriage between a man and a woman is in some mysterious way like the covenant between God and his people. G. R. Dunstan suggests five similarities between the two covenants.[8] First, an *initiative of love* creates the relationship and invites a response. Second, the covenant is *made sure by an oath*, a vow that guards the relationship against the fitfulness of an emotional bond. Third, the covenant *requires faithfulness* to certain obligations. Fourth, *blessing is promised* those who are faithful to the covenant obligations. The fifth similarity is *sacrifice*. Making the covenant requires a determination to pay its price. In both the Old and New Testaments God's covenant with his people was made by the laying down of life. In marriage, too, there is a death: death to the dependence of childhood; death to certain rights of self-determination; death to self as a whole "in order to rise to a wholeness of a new sort with the spouse."[9] ↳ leaving

The Clue to the Heart of God

Covenant is not only the divine analogy for human marriage. It is also a human analogy for the divine. It is a clue, a holy hint, written into human life to help us understand how God wants to relate to us.

Hosea, the eighth-century (B.C.) prophet, was the first biblical writer to explain God's covenant of grace by referring to human marriage. His own marriage was intentionally patterned after God's. On the other hand, God chose to reveal himself to Hosea *through* his marriage to Gomer. Hosea's marriage was a double metaphor.

God asked this Old Testament preacher to do something wildly ridiculous: he was to mimic God. He was to marry a known prostitute as a sign of God's scandalous marriage to his own adulterous people (Hos 1:2). Yet Gomer, Hosea's wife, became unfaithful again. Hosea must have struggled increasingly with the doubt that the children born to Gomer were not fathered by him for he named the last one Lo-Ammi, which means "not mine" or "not my people." God instructed Hosea to do this because the covenant formula was now turned inside out. Instead of saying, "You are my people and I am your God," he said, "You are not my people and I am not your God" (Hos 1:9). The marriage was in tatters. But was there still a covenant? Indeed there was. The house had collapsed. It had been demolished. But there was still a foundation left.

Years later God spoke to Hosea a second time. This time the message was not *about* his marriage but *in* it. God called Hosea to go and find his now-destitute, unfaithful wife and to "show your love for your wife again. . . . Love her as the LORD loves the Israelites, though they turn to other gods" (Hos 3:1).

As we read the amazing story of Hosea and Gomer, we are never quite sure when God is speaking about his own marital struggle with Israel and when Hosea is reminiscing about his relationship with Gomer. This is deliberate. Marriage for Hosea was the crucible to discover and rediscover the heart of God. Even a bad marriage, if it is a covenant, can become a means of grace. The "for worse" becomes a "for better" with the God of Hosea, and the God and Father of Jesus.

While Hosea was the first to teach the double analogy, he was not the last. Isaiah hears the Lord ask the same rhetorical question: "Where is your mother's certificate of divorce with which I sent her away?" (Is 50:1). But God's covenant love ("unfailing love") will no more be removed than the mountains and hills, and the Lord himself "will call you back as if you were a wife deserted and distressed in spirit" (54:6, 10). The prophet Jeremiah constantly used images of marriage and infidelity. Israel's sin is not simply apostasy but covenant breaking. She is, in effect, divorced, but God draws his wayward bride with lovingkindness and anticipates both the return of his bride and the restoration of the relationship (Jer 3:1, 20; 31:3, 22).

Sparing no details, either delightful or distressing, Ezekiel describes God's romance with his people as the adoption of a homeless, abandoned baby girl which, in infinite compassion, the Lord raised as his own. "Later I passed by, and when I looked at you and saw that you were old enough for love, I spread the corner of my garment over you and covered your nakedness. I gave you a solemn oath and entered into a covenant with you, declares the Sovereign LORD, and you became mine" (Ezek 16:8). The drama of salvation moves from adoption to betrothal, from marriage to adultery (16:15-22) and finally from the inevitable consequences of covenant breaking to restoration and redemption (16:35-43). But the final word is God's: "Yet I will remember the covenant I made with you in the days of your youth, and I will establish an everlasting covenant with you" (Ezek 16:60).

The covenant illuminates Israel's most fundamental conviction about her unique relationship with God. Even where the word for covenant *(berith)* is not present, the statements of the Old Testament rest on its reality.

In the New Testament Jesus both fulfills the old covenant and creates a new one. Gathering his life into one mighty sacrificial act, he said, "This is my blood of the covenant, which is poured out for many for the forgiveness of sins" (Mt 26:28). Those who follow him and trust him become what Paul calls "ministers of a new covenant" (2 Cor 3:6).

Divorceless Marriage

While marriage is almost never called a covenant in either the Old or New Testament, covenant is implied in what the inspired writers say about God's design for marriage. The most direct reference to marriage as a covenant is in Malachi 2:14, where God calls the spouse, "the wife of your marriage covenant." But the *idea* of covenant is central to the biblical view.

From Genesis to Revelation the Bible intertwines these two covenant marriages: God's marriage to his people and our marriage to our spouses. Marriage helps us to understand God's relationship to us, and God's relationship to us helps us to understand marriage. This connection is not only intentional, it is a holy help.

So what does all this have to do with the nuts and bolts of married life? Plenty. As we will see from the story of Sally and Irvine, the covenant gives us a basis for investing our energies in making the marriage work.

Sally married Irvine when he was doing postgraduate work in computer science. They were young and idealistic about their marriage and deeply in love. So far so good. They wanted a marriage patterned after God's design in the Bible, another good thing. But after two years Sally, who was supporting Irvine by her work in a bank, felt that Irvine was no longer in love with her. An incurable romantic, she had expected the continuation of the flowers and special dinners that had marked their courtship. He seemed not to appreciate the sacrificial gift of her daily work and, when he could be pried from the books and the computer, he would often go out with some friends from his class.

Irvine began to complain that she was distant and moody, overly demanding of his time and not very interested in sex. He found it hard to come home from the lab to a weepy wife. She found it hard to endure his criticisms and insults, especially in front of visiting family or friends. They kept going to church but she got more deeply involved in a visitation ministry that took increasingly more time, and he became less interested even in attending services. From her perspective, he was drifting away from the Lord. From his perspective, she was drifting away from the marriage into religion.

"Is it going to be worth it?" Sally asked the first time they came for help. "Is all the work we will have to do going to be worth the benefit?" It is a good question to ask.

Most couples come for help five years too late, but here was a couple that came at the right time, when the full reality of being married to a real person hit. They had much to build on: mutual interests, a common goal in life, a good appreciation of the qualities of their spouse, the satisfaction of having enjoyed a great deal of companionship and a common Lord. But it was not because of these assets that I confidently replied, "Yes, it will be worth it."

What gave this couple a fresh start on their marital journey was the reaffirmation of their covenant. Instead of exhausting themselves with the thought that they had made a mistake and should have married someone else, they reaffirmed that they would never seek a way out and so they spent their energies to improve the marriage they had. That involved better communication and time management, a contract for change, more realistic expectations and deep forgiveness. But the foundation on which they began to build their marriage was the covenant. They realized that the covenant was not just a truth or principle but a reality they could build on.

God's relationship to us helps us to understand marriage. This connection helped Sally and Irvine to return to God and return to each other. By renewing their marriage covenant, they renewed and deepened their salvation covenant. It was worth it, those months of talking, listening, confessing and forgiving because what they chiefly gained was not merely a happier marriage but some of the fruit of the Spirit. That's God's divine plan for marriage. It is not a contract for happiness but a covenant for the increasing satisfaction of our deeper need to have a mature character and to know our covenant God.

An Exercise

Significantly, Paul was not inspired to speak about the vegetables of the Spirit. Vegetables grow quickly. It takes several years of pruning, fertilizing and cultivating for a fruit tree to bear. Instead of thinking of happiness as the instant goal of marriage (supposedly it diminishes after the first day), consider the fruit of the Spirit (Gal 2:22-23) as a measure of covenant satisfaction and the character goal for your marriage.

Take each of the nine fruit of the Spirit and consider in practical terms what it means to make this fruit as a goal for your marriage. Write a sentence about its practical meaning in terms of your life. Some additional Scriptures have been noted to help enlarge your definition. Share your ideas with your spouse.

☐ *love* (Mt 22:37-39)
☐ *joy* (Acts 16:23-33)
☐ *peace* (Rom 5:1; Eph 2:14-15)

☐ *patience* (Jas 1:3-4; 2 Cor 6:4-6)
☐ *kindness* (Col 3:12-14)
☐ *goodness* (Rom 15:14; Eph 5:8-9)
☐ *faithfulness* (2 Cor 1:18; 2 Tim 2:2)
☐ *gentleness* (Mt 11:29; Eph 4:2)
☐ *self-control* (Acts 24:25; 2 Pet 1:6)

3
Saying "I Do"

RUSSELL DICKS, A MARRIAGE counselor in Florida, provides a cynical vignette which describes a marriage that never really takes place:

Assuming that sexual expression is irresistible, like a flood, many couples inevitably find themselves standing before a minister to be married. Minister: "Do you take this woman with all her immaturity, self-centeredness, nagging, tears, and tension to be your wife, forever?" The dumb ox, temporarily hypnotized by the prospect of being able to sleep with her every night, mumbles, "I do." Then the preacher asks the starry-eyed bride who is all of eighteen, "Do you take this man, with all his lust, moods, indifference, immaturity, and lack of discipline to be your husband, forever?" She thinks that "forever" means all of next week, because she has never experienced one month of tediousness, responsibility, or denial of her wishes, so she chirps, "I do," in the thought that now she has become a woman. Then the patient minister parrots, "By the authority committed unto me as a minister of Christ, I pronounce you man and wife. . . ." As he does, he prays a silent prayer for forgiveness, for he knows he lies. They are not now husband and wife and

Herman by Jim Unger © 1979, Universal Press Syndicate. Reprinted with permission. All rights reserved.

"You're supposed to say 'I do' not 'I'll try.' "

he knows that few of them ever will be. They are now legally permitted to breed, fuss, bully, spend each other's money, and be held responsible for each other's bills. It is now legal for them to destroy each other, so long as they don't do it with a gun or a club. And the minister goes home wondering if there isn't a more honest way to earn a living.[1]

While people go through the motions of legal and religious marriage, the essential ingredient, the covenant, is often missing. And thus no real marriage has commenced in the ceremony.

The marriage covenant is that binding and bonding personal agreement by which two people voluntarily consent to belong together for good and for the duration of their lives. The covenant is embodied in the marital vows of consent, but it is actually larger than those vows. The vows are the stones and bricks of the covenant. Fidelity, what we will later call troth, is the mortar keeping the vows together. The covenant is larger than them both, but there would be no covenant without the vows. A covenant is *made* by the vows. Thus the speaking of these vows is an essential part of the birthing of the covenant. They are well worn but not worn-out.

At one wedding, it is reported, the bridegroom rhapsodized, "It is therefore our glorious and divine purpose to fly mountains, to sow petalscent . . . to glorify love, to love with love." The bride answered, "We hereby commit ourselves to a serenity more flamboyant and more foolish than a petalfall of Magnolia." Undeterred, the bridegroom came back with, "This is the purest double helix of our us-ness."[2] "For better, for worse" is a lot more honest.

Though I do encourage creativity in modern wedding services, I am convinced that the *content*—not the actual words—of the traditional vows should form the mental, emotional and spiritual framework for solemnizing a covenant. Those who have been married for some years should consider renewing their covenant with these vows on their wedding anniversary.

> I take you,
> to be my wife/husband,
> to have and to hold
> from this day forward;
> for better, for worse,
> for richer, for poorer,
> in sickness and in health,
> to love and to cherish,
> till death us do part,
> according to God's holy law;
> and this is my solemn vow.[3]

We will look now at the marriage promise in its six major statements.

"I Take You": Exclusive

Covenant marriage, like God's covenant, involves an exclusive choice. David, in gratitude for God's promise to him, said to the Lord, "And who is like your people Israel—*the one nation on earth that God went out to redeem as a people for himself*" (2 Sam 7:23). In the Book of the Covenant (Deuteronomy) Moses says to Israel,

> The LORD did not set his affection on *you* and choose *you* because you were more numerous than other peoples, for *you* were the fewest of all peoples. But it was because the LORD loved *you* and kept the oath he swore to your forefathers that he brought *you* out with a mighty hand and redeemed *you* from the land of slavery, from the power of Pharaoh king of Egypt. Know therefore that the LORD your God is God; he is the faithful God, keeping his covenant of love to a thousand generations of those who love him and keep his commands. (Deut 7:7-9; I have emphasized the

word *you* to underscore the exclusiveness of the covenant.) In our culture people get drawn into marriage, as the opening story suggests, by powerful forces that amount to a temporary mental derangement: romantic infatuation, sexual allurement and a compelling desire to achieve physical intimacy, often before a deep friendship is established. Increasingly people decide to live together, wondering whether some of the other dimensions of companionship and friendship will mature. Sometimes they go through several such "marriagelike" relationships before they decide to settle down and get married. But when they do finally marry, they have given themselves so completely to so many that they are like a foster child who has been parented by several well-intentioned substitutes but who belongs completely to none.

Another way the exclusiveness of the covenant is denied in our culture is the so-called open marriage. But this is actually no marriage at all. No marriage will succeed when one partner is open to other partners. The willingness to stand publicly before friend, family and others, and say, "I take you," uniquely and absolutely, is an essential precondition for the covenant. And it also needs to be expressed every day in the working out of the covenant. Each covenant partner needs to know that out of all the possible partners, you chose him or her.

"To Be My Wife/Husband": Relational

The Jewish philosopher Martin Buber speaks of the "I-thou" relationship in contrast to an "I-it" relationship.[4] When we relate to a person as a thing, a possession, or as someone who will perform certain roles in our lives, we treat the person as an *it*. We do not bring our whole selves into the relationship. The I-thou relationship is riskier, more uncertain, because it engages the whole person. By speaking "thou" rather than "it" to someone, we bring into existence something that was not there before, namely, the relationship.[5]

This relationship does not exist apart from the meeting of the I and thou—which sounds perfectly obvious until you think about it. It is only as we continue to meet, relate and speak that the other person can be a thou.[6] Undoubtedly many Old Testament marriages were of the I-it variety but that was not by God's design.

Buber has grasped the relational essence of a covenant, though he does not use the word. Marriage is not a contract which spells out our obligations and expectations for behavior and which can be broken when the terms are not met. A covenant spells out the nature of the I-thou relationship, which exists no matter what people do or don't do, provided there is an I and a thou.

"You shall be my people; I will be your God" is an I-thou relationship between "my people" and "my God." In the same way "my wife" and "my husband" express an I-thou relationship. The most dreaded words God could say to his wayward people were, "You are not my people, and I am not your God" (Hos 1:8). To treat God as an "it" is an invitation for him to treat you the same way—which can only lead to judgment and wrath. But God did not give up his unique relationship with his people. It was against his nature to disown his own family. He was in a covenant with them (as he is with us).

If we could write honest vows or reality vows they might look like this: "I take you, Gertrude, to wash my clothes and cook my meals, to meet my sexual needs, to beautify my life and to assist me in the development of my professional career." "I take you, Bart, to provide for me, to mow the lawn and to meet my emotional needs for support and encouragement." This amounts to saying, "I take you to *do* something for me." It is a performance contract.

Performance expectations are important, but the essence of

marriage is different. It is not "to do" but "to be." It is not a performance contract but a relational covenant. Marriage is what you *become* together. God did not choose Israel, nor Jesus the church, primarily to get his work done on earth. God chose us because he loves us. In so choosing he desires more than we relate to him than that our behavior be flawless. That is the story of the gospel and the meaning of "justification by faith" (Gal 2:16).

In the familiar parable of the prodigal son, it is the elder brother who accidentally reveals the notion of contract. He felt that he had an unwritten agreement with his father by which, in return for his hard work and good behavior, he would receive certain rewards:

"All these years I've been slaving for you and never disobeyed your orders. Yet you never gave me even a young goat so I could celebrate with my friends. But when this son of yours who has squandered your property with prostitutes comes home, you kill the fattened calf for him!"

"My son," the father said, "you are always with me, and everything I have is yours." (Lk 15:29-31)

For the father, relationship was more significant than behavior. They belonged, and that belonging was not a reward for services rendered. The younger son came home repentant, expecting only to get hired as a servant; but he discovered and relished the grace that allowed him to belong in spite of his performance. God prefers relationship to behavior. That is the scandal of the gospel and the scandal of the covenant.

As I said in the last chapter, the concept of covenant *includes* the idea of a contract, but they are not the same. Before we are to do, we are to be. Before there are covenant obligations and demands, there are to be covenant relationships. It is I and thou, not I and it. It is the Father's gracious word "You are always with me." It is Christ saying to his bride, "You are mine!" It is the church as Christ's bride saying, "We are members of his body, *of his flesh and bones*" (Eph 5:30)—words which, whether a well-validated text or not, are a truthful allusion to Genesis 2:23. As Shakespeare put it in "The Phoenix and the Turtle," "either is the other's mine." But saying it is not enough.

"To Have and to Hold": Total

"We were married before God." What Jack meant, when he began to pour out his story, was that he and his lover were unable to get married a year ago because his own divorce had not yet gone through. He had fallen in love with Janet at work. Since he could not legally marry her, they had agreed to live together. Now that the infatuation phase was well past and his two children from the first marriage were complicating his life, he was seriously considering whether he could remain in the new relationship.

"Are you *actually* married to Janet?" I asked.

"I think so," he said. But they weren't.

In marriage two people agree to belong together in every way two people can: socially, emotionally, spiritually, sexually *and legally*. The legal ceremony, in our own society at least, requires forethought, preparedness, public recognition and counting the cost. In some societies, where there is no legal registration or license for marriage, two people could be fully married without a paper document. But in those societies there is something equivalent: agreements between families that are publicly witnessed, a ceremony before the elders of the village or some other vehicle that announces publicly the new relationship. It is a deep social instinct because society has always known that marriage and the fruit of marriage, children, will have implications far beyond the couple.

The Bible says little of what is required to make a marriage legal. In fact, not a single verse in the Bible says that two people, to be fully in covenant marriage, must present them-selves before a state or political authority or before a religious official. The word *marriage* isn't even in the vocabulary of the Old Testament. To get married was simply "to take a wife." The New Testament reflects the custom of Jesus' day, which was concerned with bride price, betrothal (a legal agreement be-tween the families which was witnessed), and the wedding feast itself.[7]

What the Bible lacks by way of specific texts regarding the legal aspects of marriage it makes up in abundant teaching concerning the nature of the relationship. God's design for marriage is given in Genesis 2: "For this reason a man will leave his father and mother and be united to his wife, and they will become one flesh. The man and his wife were both naked, and they felt no shame" (vv. 24-25). Three dimensions of the covenant are suggested by this text: that the covenant is public, personal and private.

1. *Leaving Father and Mother.* This is more than leaving home. For parents it means releasing their claim to their chil-dren, and for children it means a full consent to be released. The giving away of the bride or, in some modern services, "the affirmation of family ties," is an important emotional dimen-sion of the wedding ceremony. *This is the public covenant,* and in our society it must be witnessed and registered to be legal.

2. *Cleaving.* This involves a relationship that is exclusive, special and reciprocal. *This is the personal covenant.* Walter Trobisch in *I Married You* calls this the friendship part. We could think of it as a covenant of friendship like that between David and Jonathan.

3. *Becoming One Flesh.* This refers to the sexual consumma-tion of the marriage. *This is the private covenant.*

If any of these three constituent elements is permanently missing, there is no full covenant of marriage. You cannot "try" marriage any more than you can try to be a member of someone else's family. You are either married or unmarried—or pretending.

What makes the public ceremony so significant is not whether it takes place before a justice of the peace or a minister in the church. Christian marriage does not require a church, or even Christians for that matter! God's design for marriage—leaving, cleaving and one flesh—is given to society, not to the church.[8] The church cannot, of course, require a not-yet-Christian to live by full biblical standards. And the state must regulate divorce laws, for instance. However, if Christians with God's view of covenant marriage allow society to reduce marriage to a legal contract with various escape clauses, they are depriving society of what it desperately needs for the security of its children and the dignity of its persons.

In this matter we do not break God's Word. We break ourselves against God's Word. While the church must not aspire to be the judge of society, it must not be less than the conscience of society. We do this by upholding marriage characterized by totality: to have and to hold, from this day forward.

"For Better, for Worse, For Richer, for Poorer, In Sickness and in Health, To Love and to Cherish, Till Death Us Do Part": Indissoluble

George Bernard Shaw once said, "When two people are under the influence of the most violent, most insane, most delusive, and most transient of passions, they are required to swear that they will remain in that excited, abnormal, and exhausting condition continuously until death do them part."[9] Shaw is wrong on two points. First, the vows call us to faithfulness, not to permanent infatuation. Second, the vow for permanence should *never* be made under the influence of infatuation. That is one reason why, in our society, two people should have a long courtship before marriage. But we don't solve the problem by weakening the vows.

If there is no "for worse," "in sickness" or "for poorer" in the covenant vows, then there is no covenant. I've witnessed some vows that amounted to sentimental mush, and I say that as a convinced romantic. Covenant vows are tough, and because they are tough they are strong. We cannot guarantee perpetual happiness for someone else, or even for ourselves, especially as the years go by. Happiness, like so many other good experiences, is a by-product of something better than happiness: companionship, security, fidelity and that twentieth-century no-no, sacrifice. What we can guarantee to one another, indeed what we must when we make a covenant, is that no circumstance will make us break the bond. Every marriage sooner or later touches the stern realities of a "for worse," and they are the proving fire of how truly we took our vows.

Addressing a group of medical students on the biblical reason for treasuring fetal life, I discovered what I have come to call unconscious hypocrisy. Approaching me after the talk, a student said, "I used to believe exactly as you do—until I got pregnant!" That is no different from saying you believe in a divorceless marriage "as long as everything works out."

What we need when we make our vows (or later, since now is not too late for some) is a conscious will and decision *to work everything out.* Commitment is a big word today. But covenant is a bigger word. Covenant keeps us together even when commitment wears thin. That's the difference between saying "I do" and saying "I'll try."

"According to God's Holy Law": Sacred
Whom does God join together? Does he promise to join only

two Christians who make their vows before a minister? The Bible forbids a Christian to marry a non-Christian (2 Cor 6:14-18; 1 Kings 11:1-4). They could not be married "as God's word doth allow" even if they were married by a bishop. But what if two Christians, properly wedded in church, have personalities that are incompatible? And could God join together two not-yet-Christians or two atheists?

Because God did not give marriage to the church but to society, two pagans who do not even know God's name might enjoy the mysterious grace of marriage because they fulfilled God's law with regard to marriage: *they made a covenant for life to belong together and to bless each other unconditionally.* That is why I prefer to speak of Christians in covenant marriage than of Christian marriage. Believers do not have a monopoly on the covenant, thank God!

Many young adults today skip marriage and live together. It fits the self-serving orientation of our culture. Some of the more thoughtful ones honestly believe "trial marriage" is the best preparation possible for a healthy marriage. But trying marriage is as ridiculous as trying an artificial heart to see if it will work better than your own.

Living together without being married is a stolen covenant. It is stolen not because the couple fails to register their marriage at the town hall. That is important but not essential. It is stolen because the three constituent parts of full covenant—"leaving" (public wedlock), "cleaving" (social unity and friendship) and "one flesh" (sexual consummation)—*all* need to be present in the relationship. It is simply false to pretend that one can choose to accept one or two aspects of the covenant and ignore the rest. Two people living together, or discreetly spending late evenings in each other's apartments, are stealing the blessings of the covenant without accepting the attendant obligations of full public commitment: legal, social, relational, spiritual and physical.

It is stolen covenant because two people are taking things that do not belong to them. God has ordained that the blessings of the covenant are for those who have made a covenant and accept its obligations. "Stolen water is sweet; food eaten in secret is delicious!" (Prov 9:17). But in the end we have stolen from our own integrity and personhood, and the fruit will wither too.

Quite apart from the moral issue, researchers are discovering some innate disadvantages to the arrangement. People who enjoy the short-term benefits of an active sexual relationship are hard pressed to know their intentions, or their partners', for long-term commitment. Studies done by Walter R. Schrumm show that the conditional nature of a living-together arrangement *begs* for exploitation to occur, with the intimacy of substantial short-term gains making it too easy to rationalize one's behavior, to overlook or minimize things that are important to building a relationship in the long run or to disregard the long-term welfare of oneself or the other person."[10]

Experience has shown that women are more easily exploited than men when it comes to living together. When people had conscience enough to feel guilty about premarital sex, often women would afterward confess, "I felt like he was going to marry me and that this was the way to assure it." Some women will not want the protection I am proposing in this paragraph, but it is in a woman's best interests never to allow a man to engage her physically when he has not proven his commitment in every *other* way first. If she loses him by saying "wait," then she has lost a man who does not love her. Love will always seek the best and will tell the truth. The sex act itself communicates "I marry you," and the life should back that up.

Love will always wait. Jacob waited seven years for his beloved Rachel, "but they seemed like only a few days to him because of his love for her" (Gen 29:20). Have you ever wondered how much love Jacob communicated to Rachel by his waiting? Some men will not wait seven months, or seven weeks, to gain what they want. They are not lovers. Nor is a woman who wants full sexual consummation as a means of getting the man of her choice.

What makes the marriage covenant sacred is not the prayers, the wedding service or the minister's pronouncement of "husband and wife," but the covenant. God's law is the covenant. Therefore no one should make a marriage vow, or imply that he or she has done so by a physical act, until that person is ready to be married "according to God's holy law."

"And This Is My Solemn Vow": Awesome

Words are cheap today. We process them rather than treasure them. When I first started experimenting with my word processor, I planned to tell my congregation that I was giving them my first computer sermon. I gave them my second. The first was swallowed in one gulp by the press of a button. My words were gone. Nothing remained in the chips of memory.

Actually words are not erasable, in spite of the illusion created by modern technology. But to create a covenant we will need to prize words: your words, your spouse's words, God's words.

The Hebrew concept of "word" is fundamental to vow making and covenant keeping. The Hebrew viewed the person as a total unity, not body, soul and spirit like three compartments in a train-car, but a pneumopsychosomatic (spirit-soul-body) unity.[11] People, according to the biblical perspective, do not *have* bodies; they *are* bodies. They do not *have* souls; they *are* souls. They do not *have* spirits; they *are* spirits. When I hug my wife's body, I hug her *person*. If I speak, my person speaks.

To give one's word is to give oneself. If our word is unreliable, we are unreliable. Behind the word stands the person who utters it. The word expresses the essence of the person. I reveal myself when I speak.

Therefore to reverse my vow would be to destroy something in myself. In the Old Testament, Jephthah said, "I have made a vow to the LORD that I cannot break" (Judg 11:35). So powerful are our words that Isaac could not withdraw the blessing he had given Jacob by a ruse and give it to Esau, whom he had wished to bless. When Esau begged his father to bless him too, he said of Jacob, "I have *made* him lord over you" (Gen 27:37). It is not exaggerating to say that, when a person speaks, that person comes out of his own mouth.

We would expect God to keep his word. But he expects us to keep ours. Jesus said simply to let your yes be yes and your no, no (Mt 5:37). When you say, "I do," do not mean, "I'll try."

Apparently God took the risk of giving his creatures the incredible power to make promises. By means of a vow or promise we commit the future to ourselves, not merely ourselves to an unknown future. This "power of promising" is given to all humans, not just to Christians.[12] God witnesses the vows made by his creatures. In Malachi when the priests were going through male menopause and exchanging their aging wives for younger ones, God says through the prophet, "The LORD is acting as the witness between you and the wife of your youth, because you have broken faith with her, though she is your partner, the wife of your marriage covenant" (2:14). And Proverbs 2:16-17 implies that the wayward wife is ignoring "the *covenant she made before God.*"

In the play "A Man for All Seasons," Thomas More, chancellor of England, is asked to approve the divorce of the reigning queen so that King Henry VIII could have a new wife. Having given his word of loyalty to Christ and the church on the matter of divorce, he could not go back on it, even if it cost him his life, which it did. In a moment of penetrating reflection, More explains, to his daughter, "When a man takes an oath, Meg, he's holding his own self in his own hands. Like water. And if he opens his fingers *then*—he needn't hope to find himself again."

It is a godlike thing to make a vow. It is irreversible. It is hopeful. It is a way of determining the future. The marriage vow is the promise of a divorceless future. We break our word only by breaking ourselves against it.

An Exercise

1. It is worth rereading the vows now, pondering each one. If you are not yet married, reflect long on any one of them that you are not ready to make. Do not make these vows until you have virtually no reservations.

If you are married, read these vows with gratitude, not because they serve as fences in a relationship that needs to be contained, but because they serve as sources of inspiration. They are our claim to the future. Where any one of the vows has worn thin (or was never made), reciting the words of the covenant can bring a deeper and more secure covenant to birth. Even now.

Discuss with your partner each of these vows and their implications:

Vow	Implication
"I take you"	The covenant is exclusive; my spouse is chosen and unique.
"to be my wife/husband,"	Marriage is a covenant of belonging, not a performance contract; its essence is relational.
"to have and to hold"	The covenant is total; it is public, personal and private.
"from this day forward; for better, for worse, for richer, for poorer, in sickness and in health, to love and to cherish, till death us do part,"	The covenant is indissoluble.

"according to God's holy law";	The covenant is sacred; God joins the covenant partners.
"and this is my solemn vow."	The covenant is awesome; we have given our word, our promise and ourselves.

---

2. Compare Matthew 5:37 with the story of Isaac blessing Jacob "by mistake" (Gen 27:1-40). Given the Bible's view of keeping our word, what do you think happens or should happen when we make our vows?

3. Discuss this sentence: "A good marriage is forged by hammer and by heat. With no vows and no promises we are likely to withdraw the iron just when it is about to be shaped."

4
Six
Loves

T HE MOST TENDER SCENE IN *FID-dler on the Roof* is surely where Tevye on the night of his daughter's marriage asks his wife of twenty-five years, "Do you love me?" Their marriage had been arranged and, as Tevye explained to his wife, "My father and mother said we'd learn to love each other. And now I'm asking, Golde, Do you love me?"

After reciting some of the ways love has been expressed over those years, Golde replies, "I suppose I do."

To which Tevye replies, in a chorus which she takes up with him, "After twenty-five years, it's nice to know."[1] And it is.

Love can be expressed many different ways. These are the languages of love. The Bible with its two languages, Hebrew and Greek, gives us a rich definition of love. Scripture does more than define *love*. It reveals the ultimate Lover and the source of love.

. We will explore together three Greek and three Hebrew words for love. For the purposes of clarity I have sharply distinguished these six words, but in fact biblical terms are best understood contextually and often have overlapping meanings.[2] Love plays a central role in the Bible. All of these loves are needed in the covenant. They provide mortar for the foundation stones.

Serving Love—*Agape*

Agape was an old Greek word transformed by the authors of the New Testament to describe the special love they had encountered in Jesus. In classical Greek it had meant "honor," but Christians used it for "love." It is love that goes out in the widest possible circle. It is spontaneous. It needs no cause. It is not the love that says, "I love you because . . ." but the love that simply says, "I love you." It gets its meaning from the way Jesus lived: "God so loved *[agape]* the world that he gave his one and only Son, that whoever believes in him shall not perish but have eternal life" (Jn 3:16).

Sometimes people have characterized *agape* love as "love for the unlovely." I think this misses the point. *Agape* doesn't see a person as unlovely. Jesus healed the leper by touching him (Mt 8:3). That man needed not only to be healed but to see himself as touchable, as someone who could be appreciated. Jesus loved him that way. Of the three Greek loves, *agape* comes closest to covenant love for this reason: It is a love that goes out even when there is no response. It is unconditional. It is love that keeps going, a love that is full of grace. It is a love that serves, that washes feet.

Every marriage needs *agape* love. But it is not the only love that is needed. Indeed, a marriage standing on *agape* love alone is in serious trouble.

Friendship Love—*Philia*

The word *philia* is easy to remember because of Philadelphia, the city of brotherly *(adelphia)* love *(philia)*. It is the special word for love between friends. The most obvious difference between *agape* and *philia* is the size of the circle. *Agape* goes out to anyone. *Philia* goes out to "people who are closely connected, either by blood or by faith."[3]

What makes *philia* so different from *agape* is that it is reciprocal. We give and we receive. Sometimes we give because we have received. Sometimes, if we are honest, we give in order to receive. But in friendship we expect to like and to be liked. *Philia* is love for the lovely. It is tit-for-tat love, and it is indispensable to the health of any marriage, since marriage is an extended friendship.

Friends like to be together and to explore common interests: music, skiing, canoeing, other people. They enjoy each other and want to be together as much as possible. Out of all the possible friends I might have and the few I do have (because real friendship is rare), I would still choose my wife as my best friend. Chaim Potok, in his gripping novel about two Jewish friends, defined friendship as "two bodies with one soul."[4] In his classic treatment of spiritual friendship Ailred of Rievaulx defined *friendship* as "mutual harmony in affairs human and divine coupled with benevolence and charity."[5] When friends share the same will and opinion in mutual kindness they have reached perfect friendship.

Jesus used *philia* as a challenge *to reach out* to someone who is at a distance. He expanded the circle of those to whom we should be responsible. He made brothers out of Gentiles (Mk 7:24-30; Mt 8:5-13), neighbors out of Samaritans (Lk 10:25-

37) and friends out of enemies (Jn 15:14-15).

Sometimes our own spouse is the one most in need of our friendship. One of the first tasks in renewing and enriching troubled marriages is to rebuild friendship. We can chatter our lives away in a superficial relationship without any intimacy or uniting of souls. The solution is not to find someone else but to make our "neighbor" into our friend. Perhaps, if it has come to this point, we need to make a friend out of an enemy. That is the new thrust Jesus brought to *philia.*

Gail and I will both have friends outside the marriage. That is healthy. But both of us will be best friends to the other. And that means that we must talk.

"Ezra, I'm not inviting you to my birthday party, because our relationship is no longer satisfying to my needs."

Drawing by Koren; © 1976, The New Yorker Magazine, Inc.

Passionate Love—*Eros*

Of all the loves *eros* is the most dangerous. It is highly possessive. It is the passion, longing and craving between a man and a woman. This love desires to penetrate and to be penetrated. *Eros* is the root of our English word "erotic" and all that it implies. It is sensual, sexual and sensational. It is safe only in the covenant. Nestled among the other forms of love, *eros* gives power and pleasure to a covenant relationship.[6]

Eros has generally been given some bad press, except by those who trade in spurious intimacy, like Hugh Hefner and his friends. For hedonists, passion and bodily pleasure are the ultimate expressions of love and the meaning of life.

It is a sad statement about our society that *eros* within a healthy marriage is presented by the media as dull while *eros* in an extramarital or nonmarital relationship is pure romance and fun. The movie *Dr. Zhivago* tells the tale of two women and one man. Dr. Zhivago struggles to love both his wife and his mistress, Lara. His infidelity is romantic, while sleeping with his pregnant wife is perfunctory and prosaic. A friend watching it with Gail and me said she had felt pleasantly involved with Zhivago and Lara in the bed scene, with its sweet delights, until she suddenly realized, "But that is not his wife!"

The Bible does not damn our sexuality. God made us with this appetite and it is good. Superspirituality says it is evil, or at least doubtfully good. But *eros* within the covenant is an endless distance from the unbridled lust promoted in our own culture.

H. H. Wolff in *The Anthropology of the Old Testament* comments on Amnon's rape of his half-sister Tamar and his subsequent revulsion in which "Amnon hated her with an intense hatred" (2 Sam 13:1-15). "The revulsion lays bare the false desire for what it is. This is what happens when love lacks completeness, when only *something* in the man and *something* in the woman become one, and not the man himself and the woman herself—when there is lack of the complete partnership which is in its very nature always exclusive." Then, quoting Karl Barth, Wolff goes on to say, "Coitus without co-existence is daemonic."[7]

The Bible thoroughly endorses passionate, possessive love within the covenant of marriage. One whole book of the Old Testament, the Song of Songs, is devoted to celebrating the bliss of *eros* within the covenant of marriage. I have graciously forgotten the dear old saint who told me years ago that only a person with a dirty mind would read The Song as anything other than an allegory of Christ's love for the church. What The Song contains is red-blooded love poems: "You have stolen my heart, my sister, my bride" (Song 4:9). It is holy sensualism, redeemed passion. But it also contains the insightful warning, "Do not arouse or awaken love until it so desires" (3:5). There is a right place for prickled sexual senses, and that is within the covenant.

Anyone who has read The Song with its frank but beautiful sensuality will understand why certain generations of Jews were forbidden to read the book until they became forty. They will also understand how explicit the Bible is about erotic love within the covenant. It is in Proverbs as well.

May your fountain be blessed,
and may you rejoice in the wife of your youth.
A loving doe, a graceful deer—
may her breasts satisfy you always,
may you ever be captivated by her love.
Why be captivated, my son, by an adulteress?
Why embrace the bosom of another man's wife? (Prov 5:18-20)

Eros is the delight of sensual celebration in marriage. It is both symbolic and healing. John White writes,

It symbolizes the uncovering of our inner selves, our deepest fears and yearning. As I look tenderly on the body of another, as I experience what it is to feel the tenderness of another's caresses and the delight of knowing that I am loved as well as loving, it seems momentarily impossible to separate myself from my body. . . . It makes sense then that sexual relations be confined to marriage. For acceptance and mutual disclosure are not the activities of a moment but the delicate fabric of a lifetime's weaving.[8]

Let me add a note of warning: even within the covenant *eros* without *agape* and *philia* is dangerous. It is a legitimate language of love, but only one. It should not be aroused "until it so pleases."

Kinship Love—*Racham*

The Hebrew word *racham* is usually translated "to have pity," "to have compassion" or "to be merciful." But *racham* means more than pity. "As a father has compassion *[racham]* on his children, so the LORD has compassion on those who fear him" (Ps 103:13). The word *father* is the clue.

Racham is the tenderness to which one is moved by a member of one's own family. It is not pity in general but a family feeling, a shared, empathetic caring. We enter into the experience of another person's life because he or she belongs.[9] What surprises us in the gospel is that God treats us, who are alienated from him, as the object of his familial love. The cross of Jesus means no less.

We can cut ourselves off from friends. But we cannot divorce our family. Even though separated we still belong. For family we will do what we can, not what we must. What makes it family is the uncalculating affection for those who belong to us by birth, adoption or covenant. This is *racham*.

Racham should be learned before marriage. No one has a perfect background, but unless one is reconciled to parents and siblings, unless one has learned to give and receive and to belong unconditionally *just because it is family,* one is not ready to "leave father and mother" and "cleave" to one's spouse. The family feelings and interactions we have known from our youth also carry over into our family-by-covenant— our in-laws. Those who are engaged will bless themselves by spending time with the family of their intended. Marriage is not only between a man and a woman, but a joining of families.

Do you have covenant capability? Check it out against this old Jewish saying: "Before a man marries, his love goes to his parents; after he marries, his love goes to his wife."[10] Your ability to love your parents may measure the love you can give to your husband or wife.

Courting Love—*Ababa*

A charming elderly lady was telling of her joy the day she became engaged.

"Can you remember," she was asked, "any particular thought that accounted for your ecstasy that day?"

She paused and then said, reflectively, "I think it was the feeling that somebody really wanted me!"[11]

Ababa is the Hebrew love that makes us feel wanted. It comes from a root word that means to burn, kindle or set on fire.[12] It is the normal word for the love between a man and a woman in marriage.[13] "So Jacob served seven years to get Rachel, but they seemed like only a few days to him because of his love *[ababa]* for her" (Gen 29:20). This statement of pure human love is *ababa* at its best—waiting, wooing and winning.

Courting is almost a lost word today, as is the old English word *woo*. Hopefully, courting itself is not a dead concept. If it is, may we unite to revive it! Courting is simply that sweet process by which a man pleads with a maiden to win her as his bride. (Today it is permissible for a woman to woo a man.) *Ababa* is persuasive but not manipulative, aggressive but not domineering, emotional but not seductive. It is the love needed to bring two people into a covenant.

God bids his preacher to "speak tenderly to Jerusalem" (Is 40:2), using the ordinary Hebrew phrase for wooing. He demands no right of response, but waits until his appeal is met by love and trust. Preaching is essentially wooing; so is witnessing. It is a warm appeal to the whole person, putting the heart before the head, though not instead of it.

The Old Testament uses *ahaba* to describe what theologians call election love, that is, the love by which God in his sovereignty elects or chooses a particular people to be his people. With *ahaba*, his courting love, God chose to establish a covenant with one particular people. *Ahaba* is the source of the binding agreement between Yahweh and Israel and between Christ and the church that says, "I am your God; you are my people."

Ahaba is the love behind the covenant, or rather *before* it. It brings the covenant into existence: "The LORD did not set his affection on you and choose you because you were more numerous than other peoples, for you were the fewest of all peoples. But it was because the LORD loved you *[ahaba]* and kept the oath he swore to your forefathers . . ." (Deut 7:7-8). Israel was "really wanted." While Israel's love for God is a responding, conditional love, God's love for Israel is unconditional, sovereign and wholly unmerited.[14]

In Christ each of us can discover what it is like to be a wanted child. The Duke of Windsor, recalling his childhood discipline in the court of England, said that his father, George V, would say to him every day, "Never forget who you are." The Christian needs to remember *whose* he or she is.

Courting love is not just for the unmarried. Perhaps this waiting, wooing and winning is even more crucial within the covenant. I once shared with a sedate British audience at a conference the value of placing a candle beside your bed to create a romantic atmosphere for love-making. At breakfast the next morning I was handed this note:

Rumours are rife this morning in the normally sleepy village of Oxford. The talk is that folk at Hildenborough Hall have received advance warning of a national electricity strike. The entire stock of candles from the village has been sold!

Courting love is part of the glue of the covenant. But the ultimate language of covenant love is *hesed.*

Covenant Love—*Hesed*

The Hebrew language of the Old Testament has a special word for love within the covenant. It is *hesed.* The word itself is almost untranslatable. Translators have used some various equivalents: "lovingkindness" (Ps 51:1 KJV), "merciful kindness" (Prov 11:17 KJV), "kindness" (Josh 2:12), "love" (Jon 4:2), "mercy" (Ex 20:5-6; Hos 6:6 KJV) and "unfailing love" (Is 54:10).

Hesed is covenant love par excellence: love that keeps and fills the covenant made between partners. Many of us sing about covenant love in church without realizing it is the inner logic of the chorus based on Lamentations 3:22-23:

The steadfast love *[hesed]* of the Lord never ceases.

His mercies never come to an end.

They are new every morning, new every morning,

Great is Thy faithfulness, O Lord.

Great is Thy faithfulness.

God is more than kindly disposed toward us. He is determined to be absolutely faithful to us as his bride, and he is equally determined to fill his covenant with us with all the blessing we are willing to receive from him.

Hesed is not just love, but *love plus loyalty.* It is not just loyalty, but loyalty plus love.

The Ten Commandments are the stipulations, the lifestyle,

of the covenant people. *Hesed* means living up to the covenant obligations. It is not just affection, but affection plus faithfulness; not just sentiment, but sentiment plus service. *Hesed* goes beyond feelings to embrace commitment. The old English word *leal love* expresses this idea. So does the phrase in the old marriage vows, "and thereto I pledge thee my troth," meaning, my faithfulness to the covenant.

James Olthuis in *I Pledge You My Troth* tries to recapture this missing dimension by reminting the old English word *troth*. That word, he argues, captures nuances of "trust, reliability, stability, scrupulousness, ingenuousness, authenticity, integrity, and fidelity. To be fickle, capricious, unreliable, shifty, whimsical, disloyal, rootless, perfidious is anything but trothful."[15] Olthuis calls us to lift marriage from the realm of physical acts, like intercourse, and changeable feelings, like warmth, to a dimension of married life that will undergird every marital experience: troth. "Physical intercourse," he says, "grows out of this *troth-intercourse* and consummates it as a good gift of the Lord in marriage."[16]

. More than any of the other loves (but not without them!) *hesed* is the mortar that holds the stones in place in the covenant. Fidelity is how we "keep" the vows. Commenting on this, Olthuis says,

In good times the norm of troth becomes a joyful reality that daily takes a couple along and leads them into new and richer experiences; in difficult times troth is a ready support that holds the couple together even as it pushes them along. In times of conflict the norm quietly but persistently reminds the couple that the issue must be resolved or it will gradually undermine the entire relationship; in times of betrayal the norm of troth is the unwelcome but firm presence that urges the unfaithful partner to a change of heart as it rebukes the couple and visits them with the dire results.[17]

We Need All the Loves

Hesed does not stand alone. It takes more than one love to make, keep, fill and renew a covenant. The three Hebrew loves work together in a complementary harmony.

Because of the LORD's great love *[hesed]* we are not consumed,

for his compassions *[racham]* never fail.

They are new every morning;

great is your faithfulness." (Lam 3:22-23)

In the familiar confession of David, after he had committed adultery with Bathsheba, the Lord's loyal love and family love form the basis of David's hope for restoration. "Have mercy on me, O God, according to your unfailing love *[hesed]*; according to your great compassion *[racham]* blot out my transgressions" (Ps 51:1). "The LORD did not set his affection on you and choose you because you were more numerous than other peoples. . . . But it was because the LORD loved *[ahaba]* you. . . . He is the faithful God, keeping his covenant of love *[hesed]* to a thousand generations of those who love him and keep his commands" (Deut 7:7-9).[18]

We need all the loves. But in marriage we need loyal love, *hesed,* more than any other. Love is relational; and if the relationship is temporary, one love can never be known. There is no instant joy in marriage, and without a binding pledge, without troth, without *hesed,* few couples would survive the "for worse" experiences, the lean periods of a marriage which are the indispensable prelude to renewal and a deeper relationship. The irrevocable covenant is not a padlock but a safety net. Because it is securely underneath, the two trapeze artists can afford to take risks with each other.

Speaking the Right Love Language

We have explored six kinds of love in the covenant. All are

needed but not in the same way, at the same time or to the same extent. They are different ways of saying, "I love you." Judson J. Swihart in *How Do You Say, "I Love You?"* describes a scene in a small village in France. A handsome young German gentleman approaches an attractive young French girl that he is anxious to get to know. Carefully choosing his words, he speaks to her—in German—but is met with an ingratiating nod and smile. She speaks only French, and he only German. Often in marriage the same thing happens. Each says to the other, "I love you," but is unheard because it is not said in the language the spouse is able to hear.

My wife, Gail, was once deeply hurt by the biting criticism of a man whose judgment we respected. There was a deep inward work to be done in solitude after that, and only she could do it. I felt helpless beside her. When we turned in for the night, I reached over to touch her. I wanted to heal her hurt by reaching out in physical affection and giving myself completely to her. But what she needed was not *eros*, passionate love, but *philia*, friendship love. She needed me beside her, praying for her and waiting in silence.

The story of Mary and Martha in Luke 10 tells of two love languages. Martha was saying "I love you" to Jesus by her elaborate preparations for the dinner. She was speaking the language of practical service, just as many husbands and wives do in their routine chores or as they bring home paychecks. But what Jesus wanted was the language of friendship, and Mary had chosen the better part by sitting at his feet and listening to what he said. Both languages were good, but only one was appropriate at that moment.

Each of the six loves we have explored is a language. All are needed. But one of the secrets of a well-glued covenant—or a well-communicated "I love you"—is to see that the right language is spoken.

An Exercise

I. The following statements for you to complete should help you discover how you like to hear "I love you" and how you can best speak it to your spouse. Each partner should fill out the sentences; then share.

1. Serving Love—*Agape* (love that likes; unconditional love). This is the language of caring. *Agape* is the love that sees the best in another and reaches out even when there is no response.

   a. When I was a child the most special way my parents showed me they loved me was . . .

   b. I know that my spouse *really* loves me when . . .

   c. I think my spouse would appreciate having his or her feet washed by my . . .

2. Friendship Love—*Philia* (reciprocal; based on likes; selective but seeking). This is the language of sharing. *Philia* celebrates the common life: common interests, common likes, common thoughts.

   a. When I was young what I appreciated most about my friends was . . .

   b. One of the things I like best about my spouse as a friend is . . .

   c. I think my spouse would appreciate my friendship more if I shared . . .

3. Passionate Love—*Eros* (possessive; passionate; exclusive). This is the language of touch. *Eros* brings closure to the covenant and power to its continuing renewal.

   a. I have strong affectionate feelings for my spouse when . . .

   b. I feel ready to be touched when . . .

   c. I think the most meaningful thing I can do to express my love physically to my spouse is . . .

4. Kinship Love—*Racham* (family feeling; my spouse, my next of kin). This is the language of empathy. *Racham* is the love that encourages us to treat our spouse as kith and kin, as one with whom we have an unconditional sense of belonging and for whom we will do all we can.

   a. When I was a child I felt understood when . . .

   b. In our relationship it hurts my feelings when my spouse . . .

   c. I think I could show empathy to my spouse by . . .

5. Courting Love—*Ababa* (waiting, winning, wooing; a warm, winning appeal). This is the language of romance. *Ababa* is the love that first seeks the beloved. Then within the covenant, the courting must continue as we woo and win a deeper romance across the spaces and distances of our relationship.

   a. In our courtship I felt loved romantically when . . .

b. The nicest gift my spouse has ever given to me is . . .

c. I think my spouse would like me to be more romantic by . . .

6. Covenant Love—*Hesed* (love plus loyalty; troth; eagerness to keep the covenant). This is the language of fidelity. *Hesed* provides the relational framework for the development of all the graces of the marriage covenant.

a. My friends have always shown loyalty to me by . . .

b. The most important thing my spouse does to show faithfulness to me is . . .

c. I think my spouse would appreciate my expressing loyal love by . . .

II. Sometimes we think we know what is important to our spouse when we do not. Which language does your spouse like best? Use the following chart to rank (from 1 to 6, 1 being the most important and 6 the least) first your preferences, and then your spouse's. Let your spouse do the same. Did you anticipate accurately your spouse's ranking? Use the results for a good fire-side conversation.

	Wife's Ranking		**Husband's Ranking**	
	Mine	Husband's	Mine	Wife's
1. Serving love				
2. Friendship love				
3. Passionate love				
4. Family love				
5. Courting love				
6. Covenant love				

5
Six
Loyalties

MY BROTHER JOHN AND I DE-
cided as teen-agers to build a speed boat. We set out to create
a molded plywood hull unlike anything on the market. It
would have both a concave hull at the bow for cutting into the
waves, and a gently convex hull toward the stern to facilitate
the planing at high speeds. We made the mold for the hull and
then placed row after row of cedar and mahogany veneers over
the mold, crisscrossing, stapling and gluing each piece until it
was five ply, shaped as we wanted it.

But before the hull ever reached the water, it had to be
destroyed. More accurately, it self-destructed. We had used the
wrong glue.

When getting married, no one intends to become unglued.

But the fact that it happens, and happens so tragically for both partners, is reason enough to make sure that the covenant is well glued, and that the right glue is used.

Hesed, the most important of the loves, means that *love is loyalty* and *loyalty is love*. They are inseparable not because they are related as cause and effect (because I love I am able to be faithful) but because they are the same thing (I could not love you and be unfaithful). *Hesed* is the best glue of the covenant. Out of troth the other loves can grow and flourish because *loyalty* is foundational to a covenant marriage.

Therefore fully to love our spouse we will need to develop a vocabulary of loyalty, fidelity or troth, to go alongside the languages of love. *Hesed* calls for no less than the six expressions of loyalty now considered

Attitudinal Loyalty

Hesed involves cherishing our spouses, thinking the best of them. This is not a game of "let's pretend." It comes from *choosing* to see them with an attitude of respect rather than of withering criticism. An ancient negative example was the attitude of King David's wife when she watched him dance and celebrate while the ark was being brought into Jerusalem. "She despised him in her heart" (1 Chron 15:29). That was an assault on their covenant.

Sometimes attitudinal loyalty is not so much an "act of faith" as the result of faith, since it requires seeing our partners from Christ's perspective. "From now on we regard no one from a worldly point of view" (2 Cor 5:16). Covenant love plus loyalty calls us to redeem our attitudes.

Doris found herself constantly bogged down with her negative attitudes toward Bob. She had good reason. Bob was an overbearing husband who, largely unconsciously, tried to run his home the way he did the office. Their marriage was an illustration of the principle that what may make for success in the business and professional world may lead to failure at home. There was a lot of work to be done in their relationship, work which Bob was not ready to do. But there was something Doris *could* do.

She could change her attitude toward her husband. Instead of concentrating on his obvious faults, verbally criticizing him or falling into a sullen, depressed silence, Doris asked God to reveal his viewpoint on Bob. In repeated prayer she cherished her husband in God's presence without losing sight of his faults. She began once again to see his good qualities, so easily forgotten. With the Lord's grace she could foresee the possibility that even those troublesome qualities were areas where great character development could be experienced in Christ.

God through his grace released Doris to be loyal attitudinally, and Doris by her loyalty was able to release Bob to be himself, at least until Christ had finished remaking him.

Verbal Loyalty

How we choose to speak to one another will also have a powerful effect on our relationship. Our speech can undermine integrity or trust and therefore erode loyalty, or our speech can be a powerful force in strengthening the covenant. Sarah called Abraham "lord" or "master" (1 Pet 3:6). Any married male who confessed his desire for this title might, today, be shot on the spot! We will see later how the Christian marriage covenant implies a gracious equality of husband and wife, but Sarah's way of speaking to her husband both expressed and affirmed a loyal heart.

How do we speak of our spouse in public or in private? Are they words of loyalty, covenant-building words, or words that will erode the foundation of our marriage? A significant turning point for one couple on the verge of separation was to eliminate from their vocabulary words that expressed disloyalty. And they put out of their speech entirely the word *divorce.*

Here are some examples of disloyal words:

☐ My wife just can't seem to do anything right around the house.

☐ Sometimes when I see my husband behaving as he did in the meeting yesterday I wish I had married someone else.

☐ You embarrass me so much in public that I would rather not go anywhere with you.

☐ In our marriage, my wife wastes every cent I make!

☐ If you don't stop doing that I'm going to divorce you.

In each case there was not enough *besed* to speak loyal words.

Physical Loyalty

Sex is more than intercourse. By nature we are sexual beings and this colors much of our lives. But in marriage we and our spouse become "one flesh," sexually committed primarily to one person. Yet it is not always clear—especially in our culture—what this entails.

Sex within the covenant is joyful and meaningful. But when sex within marriage has lost its luster or is just plain boring or, worse still, has been temporarily discontinued, then what? Commenting on this Lewis Smedes reflects that "few experiences seem more justifiable than a love affair to a person who feels robbed of all the glittering promises of a romantic marriage. . . . We need a profound reason to justify staying home nights when home is next to hell. Why stick with what you are stuck with when the bright, beautiful people of our Camelot culture are living endorsements of the prevailing hunch that self-maximizing is a lot more fun than covenant-keeping?"[1]

That profound reason is covenant loyalty. And *besed* comes with a promise of eventual blessing: the comfort of dwelling in a secure covenant, the hope of becoming a better person, the gradual unfolding of the fruits of the Spirit, and the ultimate words of our Maker, "Well done!"

Sandra and Bill belong to the same home study group as John and Marilyn. Sandra finds John especially interesting and they are often kibitzing during the coffee time at the end of the meeting. They click. John seems to meet a need in Sandra that Bill cannot. Perhaps it is because John is a more affectionate person and Sandra is very responsive to his touch whenever he hugs her. Sandra and Bill are happily married, so they say, but Bill is not sure whether he should encourage or discourage this friendship. Sandra does not feel that their marriage is threatened. What should they do? Should they do anything?

In a controversial section of *Mere Morality*, Smedes explores the fringes of fidelity. He not only observes that men have always made friends with women who excited them sexually, but he says we need those friendships.[2] I appreciate his forthrightness in handling this important topic, but I do not share his acceptance of sexually tainted friendships as normal and containable within the covenant. Frankly I think he gives approval to what constitutes a serious threat to the covenant. However, Smedes minces no words on the pharisee who claims to be faithful only because he had not been in bed with someone else. "Technical fidelity, which reserves adulterous guilt only for penetration while it winks at all the other sexual games our fantasies can inspire is complacency bought too cheaply. More important still, a friendship free and clear of sexual touch could in fact be an emotional seduction away from one's commitment to the love of a dull spouse."[3]

Spiritual Loyalty
Even more sensitive than sexual loyalty, for married Christians, can be the respect for the partner's spirituality. Many men feel burdened by their wives' expectations for them to lead in fam-

ily devotions and be the "spiritual head" of the home. When wives unfavorably compare their husbands with other men, especially with the pastor, a man may have the same feeling of rejection as he would if his wife had had a sexually tainted friendship outside the covenant. Also, many men crush their wives' confidence and independence by criticizing whatever they attempt. Every expression of a wife's spirituality is either belittled or seen as a usurpation of the man's "authority."

Maureen and David became Christians rather late in life, just when David was retiring from teaching at the university. Maureen had always thought of herself as more intuitive and sensitive than David, qualities which David affirmed and appreciated, at least until they both became spiritually alive. Then it seemed that Maureen grew by leaps and bounds. In her private devotions she experienced great release in prayer and praise. In public she would often have deep insight into people's hearts, while David seemed to be content with doing practical chores in the Christian fellowship. He felt he was more "down-to-earth"; she felt she was more "spiritual."

What grieved Maureen most was that she kept looking to David for spiritual leadership in the marriage. She expected him to take the lead in reading the Bible and praying together. She believed he should be able to share deep things he had discovered in his personal meditations, and he rarely did.

What grieved David was the increasing superspirituality of his wife and the unspoken criticism of his own spirituality that daily hung over their home like a dark cloud. Probably Maureen was not any more advanced in Christ than David. They were just different.

Health came to the spiritual friendship the day Maureen was converted to spiritual loyalty to her husband.

She said, "The day I stopped trying to make David the head of the home, released him to be a Christian his own way, a wonderful thing happened. He *did* become head and began to minister to me, not the way I thought he should, but the way he could."

Knowing these two, one would be hard pressed to say one was more mature than the other. Most differences in spiritual maturity are more imagined than real. But full partnership in marriage requires loyalty to your spouse's genuine spirituality, whatever that is. Chances are, it is what you really need.

Decisional Loyalty
Decision making is another area where we must express our loyalty. Gail and I try to make all our decisions together. When we cannot make them together, we wait. When we can't wait, we pray for a miracle! And when there is no miracle and we have to decide something, we are determined to be loyal to the decision *we* have made, even if we did not contribute equally to it. There is hardly an easier way to erode covenant fidelity than to undermine a decision made by our spouse, or even one made together which turned out badly. To be able to count on our partner's loyalty is a precious gift. But it is no less than what we should expect in a marriage characterized by *hesed*.

Tom and Geri were destined to have a power struggle in their second marriage. Years before they had begun to follow Jesus each had shared in the painful destruction of a marriage. But this time they wanted it different. And this time they had Christ in common. But one very human factor almost wrought havoc on their life together.

Each had lived the single life long enough to feel completely comfortable with being alone. There are some advantages in remaining unmarried. Tom could play golf with his friends whenever he wanted, and Geri was advancing professionally in rehab medicine. Once married, every morning was a battle:

who would make the breakfast? Almost every evening rounded the day off with some other power struggle, always compounded by the fact that one was more awake in the morning and the other at night. Even little decisions became the battleground for two strong personalities, until a miracle took place in their wills. Each submitted to the other. Their marriage would be fully mutual.

The test came when they gave up their primary interest in their careers to develop a new business together. It was a mutual decision. The many months of long hours, debt and growing pains in their new business gave many opportunities for decisional disloyalty: "If only you had not talked me into . . ." But they remained faithful to each other and adversity helped build rather than destroy their relationship.

Heart Loyalty
Tom and Geri were also learning another kind of loyalty: loyalty to the *relationship*, not merely to the *person*. Each made a stubborn commitment to grow in the relationship and to keep the door open to the possibility that the marriage can get better. Their relationship became more important than their careers, their business and their personal happiness.

Troth means saying, "We will work it out. We will never solve a marriage problem by leaving the marriage. Indeed, we cannot. There is an elastic joining of our hearts, a net beneath us, a heavenly hand holding us."

These languages of loyalty are just ways of expressing troth. It may be useful to discuss with your intended or actual spouse the language most in need of improvement in your relationship.

Without love, loyalty might become a tiresome duty. Without loyalty, love might become a spent force that needs to be artificially stimulated. Love without loyalty leads to an insecure covenant, even a situational covenant. Loyalty without love leads to an empty covenant. Together they are the glue of the covenant, the mortar holding together the stones of the marital foundation. Andre Maurois put it this way: "I bind myself for life; I have chosen; from now on my aim will be, not to search for someone who will please me, but to please the one I have chosen."[4]

An Exercise

Complete the following statements to help you discover how you (and your spouse) need to hear "I am loyal to you" and how you can best speak this message. This is an exercise on *besed,* love that is loyal. Each partner should fill out the sentences; then share.

1. Attitudinal loyalty

a. I feel that my spouse has a loyal attitude toward me when . . .

b. I noticed my spouse had a disloyal attitude toward me when . . .

c. It will help me to encourage my spouse in my attitude if I . . .

2. Verbal Loyalty

a. The words which my spouse uses to communicate loyalty best to me are . . .

b. The most significant thing I can do in my speech to communicate loyalty is . . .

3. Physical loyalty

a. What I would most like to talk about to my spouse in order to build loyalty in this area is . . .

b. What I can do to express and build reassuring fidelity in this sensitive area is . . .

4. Spiritual loyalty

a. I feel that my own relationship to God and Christian life is considered subchristian when my spouse . . .

b. The most significant thing I can do to renounce playing the pharisee (I am holier than thou) or the publican (you are holier than I am) is . . .

c. I think my major spiritual contribution to the relationship is . . .

5. Decisional loyalty

a. A recent example of how I sabotaged (or attempted to) a decision "we" made is . . .

b. One step I can take toward increasing our confidence in shared decision making is . . .

6. Heart loyalty

a. In our marriage I feel that loyalty to the relationship is most threatened when . . .

b. I can better express to my spouse my decision never to leave the marriage and always be ready to work for growth, or to be open to change, by . . .

Part Two:
Building
the Marriage

6
The Ten Commandments of Marriage

BILL, IF I SHOULD PASS AWAY BE-fore you, do you think you would marry again?"

"I suppose I would," Bill replied.

"I hope you don't mind my asking," said Jennifer, "but if you did remarry, would you let your new wife have my Mercedes?"

"Actually, as you know, it's been a superb car, and the mileage is still quite low. Yes, I think that would be a good idea. As long as you wouldn't mind."

"Of course not. And my new fur coat?"

"Honey, now you are getting personal. But when you think about it logically, if it did fit, it would not be good stewardship to try and sell it. It's hardly been worn."

"And my golf clubs?"

"No, she's left-handed."

The unintended self-revelation tells it all. Faithfulness, what Olthuis calls troth, is not merely outward loyalty. It is having no one else in mind. The covenant requires no less.

The Obligations of the Covenant

Most people shrink from "obligations." They much prefer "freedoms." For instance, in modern marriages many couples want all the benefits of the covenant without the obligations. But the biblical concept of covenant simply doesn't work that way. *While the covenant itself is unconditional, the blessings of the covenant are conditional.*

That is where law comes in. In the Old Testament, especially in the Sinai covenant, God unconditionally adopted the Hebrew slaves as his own people (Ex 19—20). Then he spelled out the obligations of that covenant in terms of the Law and the cultus (all the worship requirements). The Law was to be the appropriate lifestyle of those who were in covenant.

Law: A Lifestyle. Law is almost a dirty word today. One secular cartoon shows Moses descending from Mt. Sinai with the tablets in his hands. The caption reads, "It's only the first draft, but I can tell you that you're not going to get away with anything!" Another has Moses saying to Aaron, "I have some good commandments and I have some bad commandments."

But these cartoons have missed the point. Why would any of the commandments be bad? Hard, yes; but not bad. In the Old Testament covenant, God graciously provided a way of forgiveness when the commandments were not kept, at least when there was no deliberate, willful transgression. In the new covenant the blood of Jesus brings us forgiveness and heals our bruised consciences (1 Jn 1:7).

The obligations of the covenant are not there to restrict our joy and delight in belonging. Rather, they demonstrate appropriate ways of behaving. They are invitations to experience the covenant's blessing.

It *appears* in Exodus 19:4-5 that being God's people is conditional on keeping the law and worshiping God, that the covenant is a vicious circle: God chooses me, *but to be really his* I must perform my obligations. But, as Gordon Wenham so carefully shows in *Law, Morality and the Bible,* what looks like a vicious circle is really a gracious circle. It brings the covenant partner to a fuller appreciation of the benefits of her election and salvation. Wenham puts it this way: "Law both presupposes and is a means of grace."[1] That is how we are to understand the blessings and the curses that go with the Law (Deut 27:9—29:9).

Law: A Means of Grace. The law is not what we have to do in order to be God's people. Many today believe they cannot belong to God because they have broken this or that law. They have misunderstood the Bible. The law is the lifestyle of those *who already belong.* It is spiritually essential to see the whole

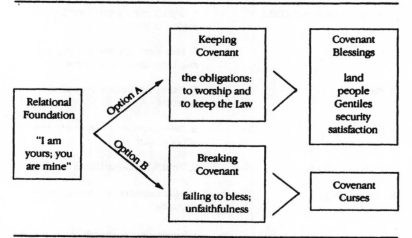

Figure 1. The Unconditional Covenant

Old Testament legislation as the total ordering of life, as a love response to God's unconditional choosing of us.[2] It is in that context that God commands us to love him. Normally love cannot be commanded, but this command is for our good, and love is evoked from us by God's own love for us.

Figure 1 illustrates the flow of biblical covenant. The movement of grace is always from who you are in God to what you must therefore do. When you have done what you ought, you are ready to enjoy the fruit of obedience.

Covenant between Israel and Yahweh	Covenant between Wife and Husband
1. No other gods	1. Exclusive loyalty to my spouse
2. No graven image	2. Truthfulness and faithfulness
3. Not taking the Lord's name in vain	3. Honoring my spouse in public and private
4. Remembering the sabbath day	4. Giving my spouse time and rest
5. Honoring father and mother	5. Rightly relating to parents and parents-in-law
6. No murder	6. Freedom from hatred, destructive anger and uncontrolled emotions
7. No adultery	7. Sexual faithfulness; controlled appetites
8. No stealing	8. True community of property with the gift of privacy
9. No false testimony	9. Truthful communication
10. No coveting	10. Contentment: freedom from demands

Figure 2. Ten Commandments for Marriage

Marriage Laws	Amendments
1. Exclusive loyalty to my spouse	1. *Unless* it conflicts with my duty to myself to be a fulfilled person.
2. Truthfulness and faithfulness	2. *Unless* clinging to a false (or past) image of my spouse justifies my not working on the relationship.
3. Honoring my spouse in public and private	3. *Provided* my spouse honors me.
4. Giving my spouse time and rest	4. *When* it does not conflict with other priorities.
5. Rightly relating to parents and parents-in-law	5. *If* they do not make any unreasonable demands.
6. Freedom from hatred, destructive anger and uncontrolled emotions	6. *Unless* provoked.
7. Sexual faithfulness; controlled appetites	7. *Unless* my partner does not respect my inalienable right to complete sexual satisfaction.
8. True community of property with the gift of privacy	8. *Unless* having separate assets would make me better off when we split up.
9. Truthful communication	9. *Unless* telling the truth about an affair would destroy the marriage.
10. Contentment: freedom from demands	10. *But* a little flirtation is fair adult play.

Figure 3. Ten Contemporary Amendments

Our love response to God is shown in two ways: first, worship, in which we bless God; second, the law, which is how we live as his people. The first, worship, has its parallel in marriage in the different languages of love. The second, the law, is paralleled in marriage by its own "laws"—without which the full blessing of the covenant cannot be appropriated. These are not conditions of the marriage relationship but conditions of blessings within the relationship. They are lifestyle statements for persons in covenant. These marriage "laws" are the structure of the marriage house, which is built on a covenant foundation. The lifestyle laws are the walls, the roof, the windows, the wiring, the heating and the plumbing.

It is a helpful exercise to take the Ten Commandments given to Israel at Mt. Sinai and to see in them an outline of ten lifestyle statements for married people. Figure 2 lists the parallel commands as I see them.

Our culture, with its comfortable selfism, would insist on certain amendments to allow for ways out when the command is hard. Figure 3 exposes the reservations many people bring to their marriage vows. They'll keep the commands as long as they're easy.

From these amendments *may the good Lord deliver us!*

For the keeping of the Lord's covenant obligations, *may the Lord equip us!*

An Exercise

What follows is a series of marital meditations based on the commandments. Since they are both intensive and reflective, I would suggest that you not proceed with them *unless* you are willing to slow down. They cannot be skim-read. It would be better to come back to them later, if need be, when you have a period of sustained solitude. Couples preparing for marriage may find these a useful outline to prepare their hearts to live a married lifestyle.

Writing your responses on a piece of paper will help you think through the implication of each commandment. Do this first *without* your spouse (or your intended spouse), and afterward share your pilgrimage. If you do this, *it is only appropriate to confess your own sins, not your spouse's!*

Commandment one: Give exclusive loyalty to your spouse (Sinai Covenant: "You shall have no other gods before me").

1. After God, are you prepared to let your spouse be the most significant person in your life?

2. Have you allowed any other relationship to come before that with your spouse—parents, children, another friend?

3. In the practical realities of life, is there some other loyalty that takes first place in your affection and your decisions—work, personal recreation, personal development, vocation, home, possessions, ambitions, hobbies?

Application: Do you need to confess anything to God? What? Is there anything that you must confess to your spouse and seek his/her forgiveness? What?

Commandment two: Be truthful and faithful to your spouse (Sinai Covenant: "You shall not make for yourself any graven image").

1. Do you have in your mind a false image of your spouse? It could be an "ideal spouse" which you are trying to shape by nagging, by manipulation, or even by rewarding. Or it could be a poor image, based on certain things that have happened—and you will not let your spouse change.

2. Do you make an idol of your spouse by requiring him/her to meet your needs for acceptance, love and self-worth—needs which only God can meet? Do you expect too much of your spouse and too little of God?

3. While not committing adultery, have you allowed your mind to embrace fantasy partners? Are you willing to focus your sexual desires solely on the real partner that God has given you?

Application: What inward and spiritual transgressions do you need to repent of? Are you willing to ask God *now* for the transformation of your mind, and the cleansing and infilling of the Holy Spirit?

Commandment three: Honor your spouse (Sinai Covenant: "You shall not take the Lord's name in vain").

1. Do you take your spouse's presence for granted as though she/he were "just another person"?

2. Do you give your spouse private honor, affirming him/her *directly?* Do you see him/her in Christ, ultimately accepted and eventually transformed into the image of Christ (2 Cor 5:16-17)?

3. Do you give your spouse public honor? How do you speak *about* your spouse and *to* your spouse on social occasions? Do you make belittling remarks? Do you cut off your spouse in conversation? Do you show public deference and public courtesy? How do you speak of your spouse to your children (if any)? Do you speak to your spouse *through* your children or *through* his/her parents, instead of honoring your spouse with direct communication?

Application: There is room in this commandment for humor, for laughing at each other's faults and for not taking our faults too seriously. But are there specific sins of the tongue about which you need to repent and to seek God's grace (Eph 4:29)? What are they?

Commandment four: Make time to bless your spouse (Sinai Covenant: "Remember the sabbath day by keeping it holy").

1. When was the last time you spontaneously gave your spouse the gift of time—putting aside work or personal pleasures in order to listen, to enjoy and to celebrate with him/her? Do you do this regularly?

2. Do you "rest" together? How can you give "rest" to your spouse?

3. Do you see the "sabbath" rituals of the covenant as holy and beautiful: A quiet walk together, a loving look across the room, dinner together and a loving embrace?

4. If you have resisted keeping one day or one time of the week as special for you and your spouse, have you been able to make every day of the week "our day" and "special" (Rom 14:5)?

Application: Do you need to confess that you have profaned the "sabbath rest" you need as a couple? What are you willing to change to create this time? Do you have it in your heart to bless your spouse in every way he/she needs to be blessed? If you haven't, are you willing to ask God to replace your stony heart with a warm one (Ezek 11:19)?

Commandment five: Relate rightly to your parents and your spouse's parents (Sinai Covenant: "Honor your father and mother").

1. Did you freely leave home, leaving father and mother to cleave to your spouse (Gen 2:24)? Do you seek your parents' approval more than your spouse's? Do you seek your parents' counsel first rather than your making decisions together as a new family unit? Are you free to honor your own parents without submitting to them and obeying them, now that you are an adult? Have you "left" father and mother in the issues of how you raise your children, where you live and how you follow Christ?

2. Do you honor your spouse's parents, or do you privately or publicly delight in mother-in-law jokes? Do you welcome your spouse's parents in your home, not allowing them to control your home (if they wish to) but not requiring your spouse to break off relationship with them?

3. Are you prepared to work out *with* your spouse how you are to honor your parents in their old age or when they are ill?

Application: Is there some action you need to take with respect to your parents or your spouse's parents? Some attitudinal change? How and when can you do it (be specific)? Do you need to seek the help of a counselor to "leave" your parents and to "cleave" more fully to your spouse?

Commandment six: Renounce hatred and destructive anger (Sinai

Covenant: "You shall not murder").

1. Do you hold a grudge against your spouse? Do you "strike out" in words or physically, destroying your spouse's integrity (Mt 5:21-26)? Do you keep harping on some offense from long ago which is supposedly forgiven, and which certainly is by God?

2. Will you "own" your feelings and not blame your spouse for them? Will you say, "I feel anger when . . ." rather than "You *make* me angry . . ." ?

3. Do you provoke your spouse to anger (Eph 6:4) by critical comments on his/her appearance, habits, behavior, faith or actions? Do you provoke anger because of your unwillingness to change a bad habit or some habitual way of speaking?

Application: Confess your darkest feelings to God, expressing them to the only One who can truly and fully bear them. How can you commit yourself to a "nonmurdering" thought life? What are some ways you can practice giving thanks to God for your spouse?

Commandment seven: Be sexually faithful (Sinai Covenant: "You shall not commit adultery").

1. Has there been, or is there now, a fantasy or real "other" lover for you, about which you have not repented?

2. Are you faithful to your spouse in your mind as well as body (Mt 5:27-30)? Does your awareness of the attractiveness of some members of the opposite sex, normal as it is, go beyond appreciation to deliberate fantasies of intimacy?

3. Do you devalue your spouse by treating him/her as a sexual object, the means of gratifying your physical necessity rather than the one who is the object of your love and romance?

4. Do thoughts of sexual lust or perversions repulse you—and lead you to repentance—or do they hold a secret fascination for you?

5. Are you willing to engage *only* in those sensuous and erotic pleasures as a couple which *both* of you agree are conducive to communicating love and commitment? Are you willing to forgo pleasures that are not pleasures to your spouse?

6. If you are lusting, are you willing to prune your life of lust by reducing stimulation from the outside (books, films, etc.) and on the inside "taking every thought to make it obedient to Christ" (2 Cor 10:5)?

7. Will you honestly determine to communicate to your spouse your needs and longings, as well as your struggles in this area so that he/she can be a minister of sexual faithfulness to you?

8. Will you resolve never to bury feelings of being sexually ignored or rejected by your husband/wife? (Some people need the help of a counselor for this.)

9. Are you willing to keep yourself physically clean and attractive for your spouse and to celebrate physical love as a good gift of your Creator?

10. Are you willing to do anything you can to meet the sexual needs of your spouse?

11. Will you resolve never to see sex as a thing in itself (just a physical act) but to see it as an expression of a love relationship?

Commandment eight: Live in true community but give privacy

Herman by Jim Unger © 1984, Universal Press Syndicate. Reprinted with permission. All rights reserved.

"I'd let you talk more, but you're not as interesting as me."

(Sinai Covenant: "You shall not steal").

1. Have you brought everything you have into the marriage, or are you "stealing" from your partner by holding back security as a safety measure or power play?

2. Do you demand a complete community of property so that your spouse cannot make any decisions on his/her own?

3. Do you control—or want to control—the finances so that your spouse may feel that what you have is not yours together but yours alone?

4. Do you demand that your spouse conform to your lifestyle or the lifestyle of your parents?

5. Do you make sacrificial demands of your partner in financial or material areas to please your own scruples or whims—which amounts to "stealing" because he/she has not freely shared in this gift?

6. Have you "stolen" power or dignity from your spouse by being boss in the relationship, taking charge, making decisions for him/her?

Application: Will you today give back what you have stolen—house, car, money, freedom, power? Like Zacchaeus consider restoring fourfold what you have defrauded (Lk 19:8).

Commandment nine: Be a faithful communicator (Sinai Covenant: "You shall not give false testimony against your neighbor").

1. When you talk together, do you share your feelings?

2. Do you try to tell the truth in love (Eph 4:25)?

3. Do you "hit below the belt" or try to win an argument by attacking your spouse's integrity (and so bear false witness)?

4. When you experience tension, do you attack the problem or your spouse?

5. Do you affirm your spouse's insights, thoughts, perspectives?

6. Do you listen to what your spouse is saying and to the feelings behind the words? Do you bear false witness by projecting on him/her what you think he/she is saying?

7. Do you exaggerate the truth about your spouse by saying things like "You *always*..."?

Application: In which area do you need to improve faithful communication: in truthfulness, in listening ability, in empathy or in openness about your own feelings?

Commandment ten: Be content and free from demands (Sinai Covenant: "You shall not covet").

1. Are you thankful for the spouse you have? Are you coveting another

spouse by making unreasonable demands on your spouse? (This does not mean that you should not express what you think are reasonable demands for change in your relationship if it is to become more healthy.)

2. Do you welcome and rejoice in your spouse's achievements and in his/her strengths without coveting them for yourself?

3. Do you welcome the particular spirituality, spiritual gifts and experiences of your spouse without wishing they were yours?

4. Will you accept what you have and what you can bring into the marriage as a gift?

Application: Will you repent of any ingratitude? Thank God every day for giving you the spouse you have.

7
Sexuality and the Mystery of Unity

ON THE COUNTER OF A MEN'S room in a sophisticated Victoria restaurant lay the current issue of *Playboy* magazine. The title of its lead article glared up at me: "Why There Is Sex." That, I thought, is something the Bible and the Christian faith address.

I didn't read the *Playboy* article. No doubt it presented the secular hedonism of the day. That sex is for personal pleasure. That it can be reduced to a technique and explained in a manual. That nothing is to be left unexperienced, nothing to be left untried or unexplored. So the popular myth goes.

People interested in self-maximization wants to *use sex* for their personal growth. They will evaluate a sexual relationship in terms of how much it enriches their own lives. They think they understand sex, but actually they do not. We cannot understand until we, in humility, see sex as a gift from the Creator, a gift that is full of mystery.

While modern people use sex, they also deify it. Their preoccupation with the genitals and the experience of sexuality betrays that they have made an ultimate concern out of something that is less than the Ultimate One. Such is the nature of idolatry. And sex makes a ready idol:

The primitive impulse to deify sexual love was not wholly misguided; it has all the features of great mystical experience, abandon, ecstasy, polarity, dying, rebirth and perfect union. . . . It prompts between human beings those features characteristic of prayer; a noticing, a paying attention, a form of address, a yearning to communicate at ever deeper levels of being, an attempt to reach certain communion with the other.[1]

The Bible puts sex in its proper place—inside the covenant. In doing so it neither deifies nor debases sex. It leaves us with the mystery of how male and female *together* can be an image of God: "So God created man in his own image, in the image of God he created him; male and female he created them" (Gen 1:27). The Bible is not silent about sexuality. Answering the question why there is sex, the Bible tells us six things that are enough to start a social revolution, enough to leave us ashamed that we were ever ashamed of our sexuality.

Sex, Because We Crave Relationship

God has designed us to move beyond ourselves. That is the first reason there is sex. "It is not good for the man to be alone" (Gen 2:18). Adam discovered that soon enough. He needed another like himself—but different. The male by himself cannot be fully in the image of God, nor can the female. "So God created man in his own image . . . male and female he created them." We are designed for the covenant, for relationship.

The biblical phrase "the image of God" presupposes the idea of relationship. God is a trinity, mankind a duality of relationships. Man or woman by himself or herself cannot express the glory of God. We must relate to become godlike. So part of our spiritual pilgrimage is to relate healthily to the opposite sex. The Roman Catholic writer Richard Rohr explains it this way:

> God seemingly had to take all kinds of risks in order that we would not miss the one thing necessary: we are called and even driven out of ourselves by an almost insatiable appetite so that we could never presume that we were self-sufficient. It is so important that we know that we are incomplete, needy, and essentially social that God had to create a life-force within us that would not be silenced—not until 10 minutes after we are dead, they told us novices![2]

One of the signs of sexual brokenness in the world and in the church is that people see sexuality in terms of themselves, their own fulfillment, their own pleasure, their own identity. Norman Mailer spoke for many when he defined love as "the search for an orgasm more apocalyptic than the one that preceded it." Mailer has turned his back on God's purpose for sexuality. God wants to move us beyond our private pursuit to consider the other. Sex is a tool of the covenant that was never meant for "me" but for "us."

Our society is not oversexed. It is undersexed. Preoccupation with the genitals has kept us from understanding what sexuality is all about. It is the call written into our natures, a code that makes us both attracted and attractive, a sign of the truth that we were made to dwell in covenant. Single people, like Richard Rohr, may still celebrate their appetite for covenant even while choosing not to allow its full expression in the covenant of marriage. Many do this within a covenant community. Far from stigmatizing the single person, the New Testament offers singleness as a calling and a gift (1 Cor 7:17).

The mystery of sexuality is that in respecting the opposite sex, whether married or single, we actually find ourselves more completely. Paul said that within marriage "he who loves his wife loves himself" (Eph 5:28).

Reflecting on the possible benefits of genetic engineering, Bil Gilbert in a *Time* magazine essay considers how we might revise human sexuality to conform to our fellow mammals who are sexually responsive for only a few weeks once a year.

> Enormous social changes could be expected if we adopted this arrangement. . . . There would be only limited, seasonal demand for pornography, rock and country and western music. The need would similarly diminish for soap operas, poorly lighted and expensive bars, high-heeled shoes, psychiatrists and after-shave lotions. Males would not be obliged to put on unseemly macho displays, nor females to have so many sick headaches. Advertisers would not have to tell fibs about the aphrodisiac qualities of beers, cigarettes and automobiles. Able but sexually unattractive people could become TV anchors, even candidates for President, and generally suffer less discrimination. Education would become the principal function of secondary schools, colleges and universities.[3]

Compared to the easy mating in the annual arousal season, notes Gilbert, our "present courtship practices would probably seem a great waste of precious time."

But sex stripped of relationship is not what humans need. Other mammals know nothing of covenant. And sexuality in human beings, God-imaging creatures, is a deep-rooted appetite for covenant—in spite of all the risks.

Sex, To Consummate Covenant

In the Old Testament, covenants were sealed and renewed by

significant rituals and signs. The technical phrase for making a covenant in Hebrew literally means "to cut a covenant." In some covenant ceremonies a bird or animal would be cut in two and the parties making the covenant would pass between the carcasses (Jer 34:18). When the Lord made a covenant with Abraham, he passed between the portions of the sacrificial offerings, thereby sealing his promise to bless his chosen family (Gen 15:17-18). This "signing" of the covenant emphasizes that it is not an idle promise but a solemn act with serious consequences.

In the New Testament the Lord's Supper becomes the ritual of the covenant for those who belong to Jesus Christ. These rituals are like any sacraments: God communicates a spiritual grace through a material reality. Sexual intercourse is the consummation and the ritual of the marriage covenant. It is no accident that the order of covenant making given in Genesis 2 puts the consummation last: (1) leaving father and mother, (2) cleaving (in friendship) and (3) one flesh. The physical seals it all.

Biblical covenants were accompanied by both outward and inward signs. The rainbow was God's covenant sign to Noah (Gen 9:12-13); circumcision, the sign to Abraham (Gen 17:10-11); and baptism, the sign to the Christian (Col 2:11-12). These are the public parts of the covenant, equivalent in marriage to the exchanging of rings in a wedding ceremony. The outward signs correspond to the inner signs, the promises and vows of the heart. Evidently the liberated women of the Corinthian church wanted to remove the signs of their marital covenant, the veiling of their heads, as an expression of misunderstood Christian freedom (1 Cor 11:3-16). The veiling signaled that they were married. We have only to think of what it would say today if men and women removed their wedding rings as they entered a church service!

Dolores Leckey in *The Ordinary Way* says that just as the bread and the wine offer us spiritual nourishment, so in "marriage sexual intercourse is the primary (though certainly not the only) ritual of the sacrament. It is an extension and fulfillment of the partners' ministry to each other begun during the public statement of vows."[4] Intercourse is to the covenant what the Lord's Supper is to salvation. It expresses and renews the heart covenant. If the symbol is not backed by a full covenant, it is merely a powerless, graceless act.

Notice what this parallel we are drawing implies. If intercourse functions as the consummating sign of the covenant, then we had better not take it without discernment—just as we should not take the bread and the wine without examining ourselves and our relationship to Christ and his people. Paul warns us, "For anyone who eats and drinks without recognizing the body of the Lord eats and drinks judgment on himself" (1 Cor 11:29). The warning holds for our sexuality as well. If we express it inappropriately, outside the covenant, we damn ourselves and damage our personality (1 Cor 6:18; Prov 6:32). Although not unforgivable, sexual sin has greater consequences than other sins. Our whole person is affected, and the dignity of the covenant suffers.

Lust, premarital sex, adultery and homosexual practice are four kinds of sexual sin. Lust treats the person as a body and therefore reduces the covenant to mere ritual. It destroys a covenant because it cares only about self-gratification. Premarital sex (fornication) is a lie. Two people are sharing an intimacy and self-abandonment that is only safe in a lifelong covenant.

Adultery is a sin against the covenant because marriage must be exclusive and monogamous. Two become one; three cannot become one. Adultery is, as Lewis Smedes argues, an assault against life's most complete covenant, a partnership that calls for a sharing of everything one is and has in life.[5]

Homosexual acts take two halves and try to join them. But the outcome is two halves rather than a whole. It is like trying to put two left hands together. Homosexuals sadly struggle toward covenant in a lonely and unfulfilling community that was never intended by the Designer.

For each of these sexual sins there is both forgiveness and profound healing for the repentant. But each sexual sin is a solemn reminder of what intercourse was meant to be: the consummation and renewal of a lifelong covenant. It is to be a mutual blessing between a man and a woman committed to sharing their lives in every possible way.

Sex, To Keep Us Distinct in Unity
Sometimes at the candlelighting portion of a wedding ceremony I have a strange compulsion to shout, "Don't blow out your own candle!" The bride and groom, hands trembling, take the two lighted candles representing themselves and, with great solemnity, light a single central candle representing their marriage. So far so good. But then they stoop down and blow out the two candles. Do they really mean to blow themselves out? Tragically some do.

One wag, hearing the familiar line "Two have become one," asked, "Which one?" In some cases that is a rather penetrating question.

Community is com-unity. The word is made up of two parts. *Com* means "with" or "together." With *unity*, it means unity *alongside* another. It is not the oneness of a drop of water returning to the sea. Sexuality is not the urge to merge. Sexuality is the urge to be part of a community of two, symbolized by the act of intercourse: one person moves in and out of another. The differences and the uniqueness of both people are celebrated at the very moment of oneness and unity. Covenant unity is not sameness or uniformity.

In shaping a godlike creature our Creator, who lives in the marvelous family community of Father, Son and Holy Spirit, designed a creature like himself. God is the ultimate mystery of covenant unity. And Paul astonishes us in Ephesians 3:14 with the insight that every family in heaven and on earth is named (or derives its origin and meaning) from the Father.

Reverently we may speak of the mystery of one God in three persons; we know they are not merged. Nor do we merge in the human covenant. Partners should find not lose their identity. The male becomes more masculine, the female more feminine. A friend of mine says that on his wedding day he felt that *he* had changed. That day he was transfigured from a male into a husband.

We need the distinction of sexes in marriage, as in all life, to achieve community. Though society would move us toward androgyny, Christians admit rather that people come in two kinds, and relate as two kinds—sick jokes about the opposite sex notwithstanding.

Covenant sexuality has this important by-product: each person becomes more himself or herself. This happens precisely because marriage calls us out of ourselves and gives us, as a gift, a greater individual identity—a unique person who belongs to another. No wonder the French say, "vive la différence!"

Sex, Because Male and Female Are Compliments
When I learned to dance it was the old cheek-to-cheek stuff in which the man took the lead. Often he was not the best dancer, but it was a structure that served the generation well. Today nobody takes the lead. Men and women stand on the floor and vibrate to the music. In marriages the same thing is happening. Each does his or her own thing. What is missing is the sense

that each is the other's missing self.

In a covenant marriage each calls forth the sexuality of the other. Eve called forth the masculinity of Adam. Until she is created, the man is just "the human" *(ba-adam)*. Only after the woman is created is he "the man" (male person, *ba-ish*). His special identity emerges in the context of needing a suitable helper. When God created the woman and brought her to the man, Adam said, "She shall be called 'woman,' for she was taken out of man" (Gen 2:23). Adam saw Eve as a called-forth one. His cry "At last!" is an expression of relational joy. Now he has found a partner as his opposite, by his side, equal but different, his other half.

C. S. Lewis compared our sexual unity to that of a violin bow and string. Both are needed and neither can be fulfilled without the other. At the Vancouver Symphony I heard an exquisite cello solo by Pierre Fournier. But it was the program notes that caught my eye. Speaking about his technique, they said that his "left hand [on the string] plays the notes and interprets the musical symbols of the score, but his right hand [on the bow] speaks, puts the emphasis, and is responsible for the interpretation."[6] In our marriage I play the notes on the score, reading them sometimes very mechanically, while Gail puts the emphasis, interpreting the notes. It may be different for another couple. All that matters is that bow and string together create one sound without trying to make each conform to the other.

Two scriptural analogies can help us spell out our masculinity and femininity: the analogy of grace (the way we are saved), and the analogy of nature (the way we are made). The first comes from patterning our sexuality on the mystery of God's revelation, the second from observing natural differences.

The Analogy of Grace. In one sense we have to learn our sexuality. Because it follows from being in the image of God, we learn by seeing how God relates to his people, how Jesus relates to his church. In marriage the husband is called the head. That is, he is to nurture, protect, provide and lead by loving as Christ loved the church and gave himself for her.

The Bible doesn't define masculinity and femininity. It doesn't give us two parallel lists of qualities, one male and one female. That should be reason enough not to generalize on male and female stereotypes.

The Danish philosopher Kierkegaard dared to define femininity, saying, "The woman's womanliness is her devotion— her giving herself away."[7] To be loved by a woman devotedly is an awesome experience, I must admit; but in the analogy of grace it is Christ who models giving himself away.

Undoubtedly some tasks are more appropriate for women and some for men, but we are wedded to the text in Genesis that says *both* the man and the woman were made in the image of God. Both were given dominion over everything, the birds of the air, the fish of the sea. Both were to subdue creation through art, technology, business and whatever else.

We dare not miss, however, what the Bible says: the husband is to be the nurturer of his wife, and the father is to be the nurturer of his children. Every time we try to define masculinity and femininity we have to admit we are dealing with a mystery, a mystery that Paul says is a mystery of Christ and the church. But we can live out the heavenly analogy in the course of our relationships. We are called to community that is a unity of opposites, and we should celebrate that mystery, not disguise or blur it.

The Analogy of Nature. The most obvious analogy from nature is the symbolism of the sexual act. It powerfully suggests that men and women are identified differently with their sexuality—in spite of the attempt of the entire scientific and psychological community to prove otherwise. In intercourse a woman receives the man, letting him come inside her. In this act she makes herself extremely vulnerable. She is identified totally in the act of intercourse because she is being asked, as Kierkegaard would say, to abandon herself. The man, on the other hand, is directed outward. While the woman receives something, the man relieves himself of something. It means something different to the man. Perhaps it is less total for him.[8]

Drawing by Koren; © 1979, The New Yorker Magazine, Inc.

"You have a wonderful body."

In marriage it is well known that a man may give himself sexually while he is angry. Indeed his sexual act may be an act of anger. But a woman cannot. She must feel good about herself and the relationship to be able to abandon herself. Surely this is why women may complain that they feel used by their husbands. A woman needs to be psychologically prepared for this self-abandonment, not only by the public commitment of her husband to lifelong troth, but by her husband's ongoing nurture of the love-relationship. This difference in sexual identity may also be the reason behind the common male complaint that their wives do not understand their need for sexual release and expression. It is a gross but instructive overstatement to say that men must have sex to reach fullness of love while women must have love to reach fullness of sex.

Therefore the Bible is adamant on restricting sexual intercourse to a single marriage partner. P. T. Forsyth comments that "love may not be spent on the opposite sex as a sex [in general]. That would justify the widest and wildest license. It can only be morally spent on a single personality. For each the other *is* the sex in this regard."[9] Passion then serves the higher purpose of refining our moral souls.

The church too is able to produce one sound only if men and women are harmonized, if men give up their prejudices against women and women give up their competition with men. If each sex finds in the other its own inner complement, there is a richness of community that makes the uniformity of a desexed community dull indeed. Single people should find in the Christian community that their sexuality is drawn out by the opposite sex in all kinds of unique and healthy ways. A single woman or man can live a sexually chaste, pure and godly life but at the same time become fully feminine or fully masculine through accepting sexual partnership in life within the community of God's church.

Sex, To Create Children

Thomas Aquinas believed adultery was wrong because people having sex outside marriage do not want to conceive a child.[10] Most people today do not find this a convincing argument against adultery. But there is a powerful hint in what is natural, as we have seen. Face-to-face intimacy, which in intercourse only humans enjoy, is a powerful suggestion about the nature of the relationship. Similarly, natural sex gives the procreative process its own way (which adulterers are always determined to interrupt) and is a powerful statement of why we have this appetite.

Lewis Smedes says that "sex and conception are the means God normally uses to continue his family through history until the kingdom comes on earth in the form of a new society where justice dwells." It would be wrong, he says, to say that every act of intercourse must have procreation as its end. In the Genesis narrative the man and woman were in the image of God and enjoyed profound companionship before there were children. But to cut the tie between sex and children is to reduce sexuality. Smedes argues again, "Fidelity is a way of opting for the ongoing pilgrimage of a people toward the renewed family of man, a way of enduring the pain and boredom of a sexually unsatisfactory marriage for the sake of a great purpose that transcends even our rightful longing for sexual fulfillment."[11]

A childless marriage can be a godly community on earth. But a marriage which *refuses* procreation for reasons of self-centeredness is something less than the God-imaging community, male and female, that was called to "be fruitful and increase in number" (Gen 1:28).

It is seldom noticed that Genesis 5 begins with a restatement of the same point. "When God created man, he made him in the likeness of God. He created them male and female." Verse 3 says, "When Adam had lived 130 years, he had a son in his own likeness, in his own image." The image of God had made an image of himself. That is part of the mystery of sexuality: we can share in the creation of new life. The preacher of Ecclesiastes marvels at this. He said:

As you do not know the path of the wind,
    or how the body is formed in a mother's womb,
so you cannot understand the work of God,
    the Maker of all things." (Eccles 11:5)

Our society treats babies as an inconvenience, an interruption to a blissful married life or a challenging career. But the Bible says that babies are an awesome wonder. Even if the birth was unexpected and unplanned for—or perhaps even, humanly speaking, unwanted—it is the work of God, a lovely mystery. I was not a planned-for child. My mother was not well enough to have a child when I was conceived. I didn't know that until I was twelve, when Dad took me aside and told me the story of our family. But with a twinkle in his eye he said to me, "You were a love baby." Unplanned for, unwanted—a frightening possibility. But biblically all of us are love babies.

Healthy sexuality makes marriage the beginning of family.

Sex, Because It Incarnates the Covenant

There is a final reason why there is sex. It is this: God wants us to have an earthly spirituality. These are carefully chosen words. Faith has to be fleshed out to be real. The Christian message is that God became a man. He didn't become just another spirit. The word became flesh and dwelt among us (Jn 1:14). Spirit became body. In marriage, too, spirit must become body. Love must become incarnate. If in the church there are word and sacrament, in a marriage there needs to be words and touch.

Our society secularizes sex. It treats it as pure body, pure flesh—nothing more. Hugh Hefner has resurrected the body, someone said, and repressed the Spirit. Sex is demoralized. There are no sins and no sexual perversions. An article in *Time* magazine confessed, "Nowadays we have sexual minorities and sexual variations, some of them involving sexual aids and sexual toys, all of them indulged in by folks with alternative sexual preferences."[12]

The converse, just as wrong although sometimes thought to be Christian, is the problem of "superspirituality." These Christians talk about God but either live like well-scrubbed pagans, or live uneasily with the physical, or live a double life. Flesh (in the sense of physical) and spirit have never been reconciled. Sex is looked down upon, almost as a necessary evil. Earlier I quoted Karl Barth when he said that "sex without marriage is demonic." Now we must say that marriage without sex is demonic too.

In Hosea's day these two extremes were found in the worship of Baal and Molech. Baalism was the religion of the land. Cult prostitutes, like Hosea's wife, Gomer, shared their bodies with men in worship to dramatize their prayers to Baal that the land and the herds would be fertile. Sex was deified. In our own society Baal finds its expression in the cult of sexual fulfillment and pleasure, sex for its own sake. Nature is deified. Instead of man's having dominion over nature, nature has dominion over man.

On the other extreme was Molech, the most perverse expression of Canaanite worship. A bronze image was raised in the valley of Hinnon (Gehenna) near Jerusalem. The idol was a furnace. And when the fire was hot enough to warm the arms of the huge image, people would place their offspring into Molech's outstretched arms and allow their first born to be consumed by the fire (2 Kings 21:6; 23:10; Jer 7:30-32; 19:4-6). The drums were beaten loudly enough to drown the screams of the children. Sex was demonized, secularized, perverted. The life force, the procreative side of sex, was violated. The ubiquitous practice of abortion in our own society is not far from Molech. Hugh Hefner is not far from Baal.

In contrast to the sacralizing and the secularizing of sex, the Bible sacramentalizes sex. It does this by placing it in its rightful place: in the covenant. That does not mean that single people cannot be whole without sexual intercourse. As Smedes puts it, "Although virgins do not experience the climax of sexual existence, they can experience personal wholeness by giving themselves to other persons without physical sex.

Through a life of self-giving—which is the heart of sexual union—they become whole persons. They capture the essence without the usual form."[13]

That the world does not understand the mystery of covenant union is patently clear. One night in a talk session in a university lounge we were discussing sex. I remember saying that after twenty-four years of having sex with my wife within our marriage covenant, I could honestly say that it *means* more today than it did at first. One girl responded, "I can't think of anything more boring." Our society is so sexually sick that it cannot even recognize health. For me there is still mystery. I would rather live with the mystery and celebrate it than to remove the mystery and make myself less than a creature. Sex is God's good gift to the marriage covenant.

An Exercise
Expressing sexuality outside the covenant is an obvious way of hurting the covenant, our covenant partner and ourselves (1 Cor 6:18; Prov 6:32). But even within the covenant discernment is needed lest sexual intercourse become reduced to an empty ritual or an act whose meaning is not shared by one's spouse and therefore one partner feels forced.

Prepare to share with your spouse by working on these two questions.

1. What I have learned about my spouse's sexual needs and desires is . . .

2. What my spouse needs to know about my readiness to appreciate a sexual encounter is . . .

Agree on a good time to communicate to each other the answers to your questions. Then share your answers with your spouse and listen to what your spouse says. In sensitive matters like this it is sometimes important to give "feedback" about what you have heard. For instance, you might say, "I hear you saying that you do not want to have intercourse with me until we have talked for a while. Is that what you meant to say?"

8
The Problem of Headship

THE WOMEN'S LIBERATION MOVE-
ment has brought a host of spin-offs, some good and some
bad. But one thing is certain: the roles of husband and wife
can never again be the same in the Western world. Christians
cannot read the biblical words about the husband's being the
head and the wife's submitting without seeing something new.
I have tried in this chapter to be both culturally sensitive and
biblically bound. But who is sufficient for these things? Over
the supper table I asked my daughters whether they thought
I was a male chauvinist pig. One said, "Yes . . . but *you are not
a bad one!*" I took that as a veiled compliment and pressed on.

The new day has been a long time coming. In 1855 Lucy
Stone, when she married Henry Backwell, joined hands with

him and read a long statement that included these words:

> While we acknowledge our mutual affection by publicly assuming the relationship of husband and wife . . . we deem it a duty to declare that this act on our part implies no sanction of, nor promise of voluntary obedience to, such of the present laws of marriage as refuse to recognize the wife as an independent, rational being, while they confer upon the husband an injurious and unnatural superiority.[1]

Not many people today want different vows for the bride and

Herman by Jim Unger ® 1979, Universal Press Syndicate. Reprinted with permission. All rights reserved.

"That bit about 'Love, honor and obey.' Is that me or her?"

the groom. At least they say they want the same vows. Herman's confusion about "that bit about 'love, honor and obey'; is that for me or her?" is typical of the day. I have been following the vows used in the 1980 revision of the Anglican Prayer Book. In this latest edition there are different vows for men and women, for those who wish. *Option A* has both the groom and bride say, "to love and to cherish." *Option B* invites the groom to say "to love, cherish *and worship*" and the bride to say, "to love, cherish *and obey*."[2] Take your pick.

Headship, a Hot Issue

The covenant has its political dimension, and the "headship debate" has raised this issue to the level of do-or-die truth. Is the husband head *over* the wife? Or are they mutually submissive marriage partners with no distinctive roles and no sex-type differences except the genitals?

Those of us who do marriage counseling realize that many marriages are struggling desperately at just this point. Some men insist that the Bible makes them responsible to God for the family. They are boss. Some women believe this is true and try for years to submit to a weak man or a tyrant. But there comes a day, almost inevitably, when the woman revolts. She may revolt by having a nervous breakdown, by getting a plane ticket and flying away, or by leaving him for another man. Such couples pose a question by their politically interpreted relationship: Is Christ's headship over the church reflected by a marriage in which the husband has power and authority over his wife?

Other couples are infected with the needle of egalitarian mutual submission. They want *no* husband or wife roles. Roles are phony, unnatural habits. These Christians emphasize that Paul in Ephesians 5 when he talks about the husband as "head" and the wife's "submission" prefixes the discussion with the exhortation "submit *to one another* out of reverence for Christ" (Eph 5:21). These modern roleless, career-matched couples pose an important biblical question: Does the husband show in parable form something of Christ's relationship to his bride, the church?

I knew that I had to write about this the day a young man, recently married, invited me out for breakfast. Mark had a problem. "How," he said, "can I get my wife to submit to me?" It never seemed to occur to him that in the Bible the husband is never called to make his wife submit. But I was driven to biblical research by an infuriating statement in a recent reputable commentary on 1 Peter. Commenting on the statement that a wife should have the "unfading beauty of a gentle and quiet spirit" (3:4), the scholar suggested that this is gained as a "wife submits to her husband's demands and intrusions *by docile and gentle co-operation.* . . . She shows no sign of rebellion or resentment, fuss or flurry."[3] I for one do not want a docile wife!

In a society which has made the quantum leap from "Adam's rib to women's lib" in two short decades, it is almost impossible to approach the subject without bias. "How do you live with a sort-of liberated male?" asks one secular writer. "Positioned somewhere between macho and sharing, this new breed of mate brings his own set of challenges."[4]

A few years ago I dared to speak on Ephesians 5 in a congregation. The sermon title had to be phoned in to the local newspaper for the Saturday evening ad. When asked what I would be speaking on, I said: "Will Liberated Wives Produce Subordinated Husbands?" The woman on the other end yelled into the telephone, "NO!"

The debate among Christians is between those who believe that the husband is head as *chief* (that is, head *over,* as the chief of a tribe), and those who believe that the husband is head as a *source* (like the source of a stream). Both appeal to the meaning of the Greek word for "head" *(kephale)* which appears in the two foundational texts:

"The head of the woman is man." (1 Cor 11:3)

"The husband is the head of the wife as Christ is the head of the church, his body." (Eph 5:23)

The debate goes on every day in many homes without being called a debate. Sometimes it is a silent political agreement with its own payoff, working until one of the two wants a change. Then all hell breaks loose. Sometimes the marriage itself was founded on a misunderstanding. The husband thought that he would be the boss. The wife thought that they would be equals and that all decision making would be fully shared. How much better it would have been if they had talked about roles and expectations before they got married!

Role questionnaires, like the one below, can help a couple before they get married to discover their expectations. There is usually opportunity to register strong or mild agreement, strong or mild disagreement.

☐ The husband is the head of the home.

☐ The wife has greater responsibility for the children.

☐ Major decisions should be made by the husband in the case of an impasse.

☐ The wife is just as responsible for the children's discipline as the husband.

☐ The wife should always obey what her husband asks her to do.

☐ The husband and wife should plan the budget and manage money matters together.

Two crucial things should happen through premarital counseling. First, each one's expectations should be expressed. Second, any agendas for power and control should be brought into the open. Headship is one of those crucial areas to be talked about. Too many people think, years later, that they married the wrong person when really they married the wrong theology.

The Heresy of False Headship

The popular idea of marriage as part of a chain-of-command has been actively promoted not only by best-selling books but by mass seminars.[5] It goes like this: God is over the husband, who is over the wife, who is over the children, who are over the servants (and usually the family dog). The husband provides a covering, an umbrella of authority, under which the wife and children are safely protected. Each "reports" to the person farther up the chain-of-command. At its best the husband feels that he is accountable to God for his wife's and children's spirituality. The wife feels that she has someone who will make her decisions and consider her best interests.

At its worst, headship as chief is a form of *control-compliance*. The husband may control by using anger, threatening to leave, using manipulative prayer or other such weapons. He may control by simply making decisions for his wife and children, and by withholding affection, money, esteem, children, communication, requests and access to parents. We should name this for what it is: false headship. Having a chain-of-command sets the family up for wife abuse and child abuse, sometimes in the sensitive area of sexuality. Unfortunately, all this happens in the name of a biblical marriage. It is a dangerous Christian heresy.

False headship is matched by false submission, or compliance. Psychology defines compliance as a psychological adaptation to pain. If I am an aggressive and angry person, I will get people to comply with my wants. Many Christian husbands conduct themselves this way, all the while thinking that they are biblical husbands fulfilling their function as head of the wife. Many are prominent Christians at church, and their wives at home are what the counselors call passive-aggressive. They control by being passive, by quitting, by dropping out, by doing nothing until they get their own way. One woman put it this way: "He is the head, but I am the neck and I turn him any way I wish!"

A wife complies when she feels she is manipulated into a marriage she did not want, when she feels she cannot express reservations about a sexual encounter with her husband, when she feels coerced but does not wish to risk upsetting the applecart. A wife complies—dangerously—when she goes along with her husband because *he* is sure that it is God's will, while all along she has no inner agreement in her heart.

Some husbands are like boiling caldrons on the verge of being tipped over. Their wives will do almost anything to keep their husbands' anger from spilling into the home, until they can keep the peace no longer. Then their own stored-up anger, until now felt as hurt, gets expressed in the relationship. Usually the husband does not understand what has descended on his otherwise peaceful home.

Even where the relationship never blows up, usually compliant persons nurture a sliver of resentment. They feel gypped, hard done by, even though they may say that everything is going fine and that they are doing God's will. What is so sad about both the controlling husband and the compliant wife is that neither is happy with the relationship, even if they *think* they are doing it "God's way." Tony Tysen once said, "When I go to kiss my wife, I don't want her to abdicate. I want a living sacrifice!"

Who wants a compliant wife or a controlling husband? I once asked Gail whether I had ever controlled her. "I wouldn't let you!" she responded. That reply left me winded but thankful. It is a sign of health for both of us.

The least damaging examples of chain-of-command are those couples who believe the husband is over the wife but who remain faithful to what the apostle says to *both* husband and wife. They are both to be submissive to each other (Eph 5:21). This takes us beyond power and control. The husband is not to think of his headship as control, power or decision-making rights. He is to think of headship as being the chief lover. "Husbands, love your wives, just as Christ loved the church and gave himself up for her" (Eph 5:25). The husband is never given the right to make his wife submissive. He is only told what *he himself is to do with his headship.*

Similarly, the wife is not told to expect her husband to love her sacrificially. ("Why doesn't my husband love me more?" I can hear someone asking.) The wife is told to view her husband as head over her and to respect, reverence and submit to him as though he were the Lord Jesus (5:22). The husband then is responsible for his wife as head, and the wife is to reverence him. But there is a flaw in the equation, as we shall see.

The Heresy of No Headship at All
In our society it is a grievous sin to be unequal. Rampant egalitarianism and selfism promote marriages that are not sex-typed, where roleless partners match career goals. Each "spouse" (the title "husband" or "wife" is obsolete in such a marriage) must be allowed "to be," whatever that means. Mutual self-development becomes the uppermost priority of the relationship. In its worst form there is no covenant at all. Two people contract to stay together as long as the relationship is beneficial to both parties.

Those who approach this spouse-spouse relationship from a Christian perspective are anxious to show that the Greek word for "head" can mean "head *as source,*" like the source of a stream. They argue—rightly—that when Paul calls the husband to be head he is *under* his wife to serve her needs, sacrificially giving himself, just as she, in this relationship of mutual submission, will go *under* her husband in meeting his needs and developing his talents and interests to their full potential. It looks so thoroughly Christian except for one fatal flaw: headship becomes meaningless.

I am concerned with what this issue does to the covenant. We have seen over and again that a covenant is never primarily a contract based on performance, duties, obligations and powers. It is true that covenants were used in the Near East to make agreements between political powers, treaties in which one king would rule over a subjugated king and his kingdom. But the covenant when applied to marriage goes beyond politics. It is primarily a relationship of belonging.

The marriage covenant is made between *equals*. The text of Genesis 2 assures us that while husband and wife are different, they are one, and one as equals. Nothing in the phrase "helper suitable for him" suggests inequality (Gen 2:18). In fact, the lexicon defines the phrase this way: "a help corresponding to him, i.e., equal and adequate to himself."[6] The hierarchical model preserves the male/female difference but makes husband and wife unequal. The mutual submission model without headship preserves the equality but denies the difference.

This last problem would not be serious (provided that both partners agreed to a headless marriage) except for the biblical presentation of God's design for the marriage covenant. It is a covenant in which the husband is the head "as Christ is head of the church." We must turn to the question of what "head" means.

The Debate Goes to School
One used to be able to settle a little interpretive skirmish by

opening up the best available Greek lexicon (which explains the meanings of Greek words) and there discover what a word means. The problem we now face is that the most widely used lexicon today, Bauer's, tells us that *head* means both "head as chief" and "head as source." Further, Bauer argues that, in those very passages where marriage is the issue, the proper meaning is head as chief or "superior rank." In this context Bauer compares the superior rank of Christ over all creation with the husband's superior rank over his wife: "God the *kephale* [head] of Christ, Christ the *kephale* of the man, the man the *kephale* of the woman" (1 Cor 11:3).[7] The husband then is chief of the family tribe. He is president of the corporation. He is priest of the family. He is the one to make the decision when all else fails (and sometimes before). He is where the buck stops.

It used to be that the argument would be settled by such a simple word study. But not today! Careful exegetes are now questioning whether Bauer understood the way in which *kephale* was used and understood in Greek society when the New Testament was written. Their study has taken them to authoritative studies on the Greek language done by Liddell, Scott, Jones and McKenzie back in 1843. Since this basic resource in the Greek language was written before the women's liberation movement, it has not been tainted with egalitarian ideas, or reactions to those ideas.

Such studies of *kephale* have brought out a richer understanding of headship than the two views that are in opposition today. Here are some of the figurative meanings of "head" in the New Testament and their likely contexts:

1. Source of life (Col 2:19; Eph 4:15)
2. Top or crown (Col 2:10; Eph 1:20-23)
3. Source, base or derivation (1 Cor 11:3)
4. Exalted originator and completer (Col 1:18)

5. One who brings completion (Eph 5:23)[8]

But a word study is not sufficient to discover what headship means. We must look at the context of the word, especially in the two crucial passages, 1 Corinthians 11 and Ephesians 5. It is sometimes argued that the 1 Corinthians 11 passage is a series of authority relationships. "The head of every man is Christ, and the head of the woman is man, and the head of Christ is God" (v. 3). Let's look at three headship models more closely.

1. God, the Head of Christ. James Hurley in *Male and Female in Biblical Perspective* argues that 1 Corinthians 11:3 presents a series of authority relationships that can be graphed as a chain-of-command:

God (the Father)
  over (or "head of")
Christ (the Son)
  over (or "head of")
the Man (or husband)
  over (or "head of")
the Woman (or wife)[9]

But what does this do to our view of Christ? God and Christ were certainly not unequal in the mysterious unity of the Trinity. Jesus could say, "I and the Father are one" (Jn 10:30). The Jews who heard Jesus say this understood that it meant complete equality with the Father (v. 33). At one point Jesus said, "I proceeded and came forth from God" (Jn 8:42 RSV). He derived his life from the Father who glorified himself in the Son. The Father completely revealed himself to the Son, but the Son was free to make his own decisions. Revelation and response was the way they related. It was entirely unlike a chain-of-command.

In 1 Corinthians 11:3 Paul is more likely giving us a series of comparisons. The God-Christ relationship is like the Christman relationship which is like the husband-wife relationship. There are both parallels and differences in the comparisons being made. Unless we appreciate the differences, we will impose on the husband-wife relationship a command/authority structure that does not exist in the God-Christ relationship.

One common element in the series is the matter of giving glory. Each is glorified (or given dignity) by being in right relationship: The Father is glorified in the Son. Christ glorifies himself in his bride, the church. There is a special sense in which the wife brings glory to her husband by recognizing his place in her life (1 Cor 11:7). Giving glory is not a matter of over/under, or rank, but a matter of appropriate relationship and of giving honor.

Or take the matter of authority. The primary issue in the series is not authority *over,* but what each *does* with his authority. The Father has given all his authority to the Son (Mt 28:18). Christ gave authority in his name (and through his Spirit) to the disciple community, to the church (Mt 18:18; Jn 10:23; 15:15). Similarly the husband is not the head by keeping his authority to himself but rather by giving it away appropriately in the marriage relationship. Paul hints at this when he says that a woman with her head covered (as a sign of respect for her marital partner) has authority to minister. The "sign of authority on her head" (1 Cor 11:10) is *her* authority, not his, when she is rightly related to him.[10]

Headship means "move over," not "move down." You are beside me, not under me. That is the meaning of the first headship parallel: God and Christ.

2. Christ, the Head of Creation. Since Christ in Ephesians 1:19-23 is said to be head over everything, subjecting the whole of creation to himself, we think of his headship as rule or command. And if Christ has to bring all the principalities and powers under his control to be head of everything, then the husband, to be head, must rule his wife.[11] But in this head-ship model, which significantly does not appear among the others in 1 Corinthians 11:3, *the ruled element does not have a choice.* It is plastic to the will of God in Christ. Christ is bringing everything into *involuntary* submission.

Headship in the husband-wife model, by contrast, means relating to someone who also has a free will, someone whose inclination is not to revolt or to be autonomous but rather, in virtue of having made a marriage covenant, to enjoy a shared purpose for life together.[12] Scripture never compares the hus-band to the ruling, exalted Christ, but rather to the earthly, suffering Christ. This is especially significant for our under-standing of Ephesians 5.

There is another problem with comparing the Christ-crea-tion rule with husband-wife headship. It is true that Paul uses the Greek word for "rule" *(archon)* when he speaks of Christ's headship over creation. But he never uses "rule" for the hus-band's headship! The creation must be subjugated. One's wife must never be.

It is true that God stated the curse of Adam and Eve's sin in terms of rule: He said to the woman that her husband would rule over her (Gen 3:16). But this punishment, curse, was not what God intended or what he wants now. Even the seemingly positive statement, "Your desire will be for your husband" (3:16), placed here among the consequences of sin, must be understood as something bad. It is not here a desire for a relationship of any sort. This "desire" is the same Hebrew word we find in Genesis 4:7 where God says to Cain, "Sin is crouch-ing at your door; it desires to have you" (that is, it desires to overmaster you). Sin makes the man rule the woman. *Sin also makes the woman desire to revolt against the man, to overmas-ter him.* Neither of these drives expresses God's original inten-tion. Neither reflects the practical grace of living in the Spirit now that Christ has come and redeemed us.

Salvation reverses the curse. Instead of ruling his wife the husband is called in Ephesians 5 to love her sacrificially. Instead of being insubordinate and revolting against her husband's leadership, the wife is called to bombard her husband

Copyright 1981 Sandy Dean. Used with permission from LEADERSHIP Journal.

"Not so fast, watch out for those rocks, don't step on that flower . . ."

with submission and respect (Eph 5:22, 33). She will never honor him too much, just as he will never love her too much. Paul calls for the new relationship because he is convinced that Christ's death and resurrection have introduced a new order, a new creation and a new humanity. We are to base our marriages on the grace of Christ, not the old curse.

3. Christ, the Head of the Church. In Christ and the church we have our most important parallel for understanding marriage headship, precisely because the Bible calls us to follow this model. Christ and the church, and husbands and wives share a covenant relationship, a chosen relationship of belonging. At one point, of course, the parallel breaks down. Christ is undoubtedly superior; we don't hesitate to speak of his being head *over* his body. But the husband is not superior to his wife; he is not head over her. He cannot save his wife, as Christ does the church (Eph 5:23). Once again, the husband is never compared to the exalted, ruling Christ but to the earthly, suffering Christ.

Let's look at some positive correlations in the parallel. Although Christ's headship is with an unequal and a husband's headship is with an equal, both headships refer to a kind of priority. Christ the groom guides his bride by revealing himself—not by telling his bride what to do. Indeed Jesus, speaking to his disciples, said, "I no longer call you servants, because a servant does not know his master's business. Instead, I have called you friends, for everything that I learned from my Father I have made known to you" (Jn 15:15). Jesus refuses to control the church. He does not treat the church the way he does the principalities and powers of creation. He gives the church dignity, freedom, responsibility. He commits himself to the decisions being made by the church (Mt 18:18) on the basis of his covenant relationship with it (Mt 18:20; Jn 15:4).

The head-body language of Paul is not primarily a language

of authority but of unity and interdependence. The body enters into the life of the head, grows up into the head, is nourished by the head (Eph 4:15). Headship is not a role but a relational process. Not a rule but a priority within relationship.

Living this one truth alone, no husband would ever make a decision for his wife. Rather he would give leadership by sharing his life so fully with her that what she wanted is what he already wanted (Jn 14:13). Chain-of-command thought is organizational and structural. Biblical headship is organic. It concerns a process in a living relationship.

The Parable of Headship

So husbands and wives are to be like Christ and the church. But *how?* God has given us no script, with lines, asides and stage movements. All we have are guidelines, general directions. The play was staged once, when Christ laid down his life for his bride. But in our version of the drama we have to live out our lines in the individuality of each marriage. And it must be consistent with who we are and who we are becoming.

If we don't accept responsibility for working out our roles ourselves, we will undoubtedly end up playing someone else's role. It will probably be one learned from our parents. Or we might try to emulate some well-meaning but hard-to-copy Christians in roles that may be neither authentic nor biblical. Adopting roles makes it harder to have authentic covenant relationships. "How can I love the real you," asks Patricia Gundry, "when you are trying so hard to be someone else? And how can you love the real me when I am trying to be someone else?"[13]

We are actors in a play whose plot is clearly revealed and whose ending is too glorious to be imagined. *But we compose our own lines.* And the process of composing those lines is far more productive of faith and maturity than the thoughtless recital of someone else's composition. What God wants is not mass-produced Christian marriages but many unique parables of his wonderful covenant with the church.

To write our scripts we must first know what headship means in terms of relationship. It will reflect *the new thing* God has done in Christ. We know that in some sense the husband has priority within the partnership of equals. Paul argues this from God's design in Genesis:

1. The woman was created *after* the man (1 Tim 2:13). Something of the rights of the first-born are hinted at in this statement.[14]

2. The woman was created *from* the man (1 Cor 11:8).

3. The woman was created *for* the man. Nothing of subordination is implied by the word "helper" (Gen 2:20). The woman was made to meet the man's need because he could not cope with life alone. She was not made so that he could have another creature to rule. She is neither his plaything nor his domestic servant. She meets his need for companionship.

Then Paul stands his argument on its head and says, "In the Lord, however, woman is not independent of man, nor is man independent of woman. For as woman came from man, so also man is born of woman. But everything comes from God" (1 Cor 11:11-12). We are not to ignore creational differences between men and women. But neither are we to let them become more important than the central parable of sexuality, the parable of the grace of God. Even under the old covenant the prophet Jeremiah proclaimed, "The LORD will create a new thing on earth—a woman will surround [protect] a man" (Jer 31:22). How much more under the new covenant may we say, "In the Lord, however . . ."?

Paul is declaring that power, control, politics and compliance are abolished within marriage once and for all. The new humanity out-revolutionalizes the liberation movement by eliminating the need to talk about rights. The husband is called to renounce headship as rule and to see his headship as nurturing, sacrificial love. The wife is called to renounce her desire to overmaster her husband (or to desire his rule), and she is called to give him respect, submission and honor *as though he were head over her.* Each does this for the other not because they must but because they *may* in Christ. It is not law but grace. If the husband does not love, the wife may still give him what he does not deserve, her respect. If the wife does not honor, the husband may still give her what she does not deserve, his sacrificial love. Each will do this, not as a mutual contract but as a covenant grace-gift "out of reverence for Christ." Christ is the inspiration of covenant love.

Practicing Headship
But, you say, as a husband you are already deep into a hierarchical headship marriage. The Bible calls you to renounce rule and to "love your wife to death." You are a passive, compliant wife? Renounce that role and bombard your husband with respect. Each is to fight for the bottom of the pile.

In a covenant marriage, the husband calls forth the wife's maturity and communicates her equality. She honors him as first in her life after God. She does not let him control, boss or manipulate her. She is free to talk about her concerns and disagreements and to express her need for love. Indeed she must if he is to succeed in his headship. But it is "safe" for her to give him priority, for he refuses to use it for position or power.

If you as a couple are in a mutual-submission partnership, with no headship at all, Scripture calls you to make a difference in your relationship. You have a parable to enact, a play to write. There are theological reasons for this, for marriage expresses the mystery of Christ. There are spiritual reasons for this, because an unscriptural marriage relationship leads to a hindered spirituality and prayer life (1 Pet 3:7). And there are societal and family reasons for this, because marital patterns are meant to be with us until the resurrection at the last day (Mt 22:30).

What is good headship? It is easier to say what it is *not.*

Headship is not hierarchy. "Hierarchy" is composed of two Greek words. *Hieros* means "holy," as distinct from profane— holy in and of itself (1 Cor 9:13). *Archos* means "ruler," "lord" or an "official." It is used in the New Testament for members of the Sanhedrin (Lk 14:1; 18:18), but never of the husband. The husband is not more sacred than the wife. He is not the priest of the marriage, not if we believe in the priesthood of all believers. We should eliminate "hierarchy" forever from the vocabulary of covenant marriage.

Headship is not rule. Rule is the result of the Fall. Some rule is needed in the home, but it is something both men and women share, as Paul indicates in 1 Timothy 5:14, where he asks the younger widows "to manage [rule] their homes." Rule is loving responsibility.

Headship is not an authority role. The husband is not accountable for his wife, in spite of well-intentioned arguments to the contrary.[15] God spoke to Adam and Eve separately about their sins, but he did not hold Adam responsible for Eve's sin, or Eve for Adam's. Ananias and Sapphira were both held accountable for their deceit (Acts 5:9). The Greek word for authority, *exousia,* means "the right and power to make decisions on behalf of another." It is used almost exclusively of Christ's authority and that of the apostles. It is used once for the woman's authority to minister when she is rightly related to her husband (1 Cor 11:10). But *exousia* is never used for the husband's headship.

Now we are ready to say what headship *is.*

Headship is being *first in a relationship of equals*, side by side but not head over.

Headship is being *first in honor*. The husband is to be a little more responsible for the relationship—which is very different from being responsible for his wife.

Headship is being *first in nurturing, loving and building the relationship*. The husband is to be concerned for his wife's needs, her sanctification and her growth as a person. He is to be more concerned that she is fulfilled than that he is!

Headship means being *first in initiation*. The wife is free to take initiative too, but the husband has priority in initiation.

Headship is being *first in providing for the wife and children*. This is not just food and shelter but includes the emotional needs of the family. If the wife has a unique role in procreation (1 Tim 2:15), the husband has a unique role in provision. The man's vocation may shape where and how the family lives, even if both choose to work. But the husband, by being willing to sacrifice himself for his wife, will see that her calling and vocation are fulfilled too. This is not a rule, however: there are important exceptions where the husband is unemployed, for instance, and the wife is able to support the family.

Headship is a high calling. But in writing the lines of our play in the intimacy of our own marriages, we are drawn into the very mystery of God. It is an act of worship, and the Spirit of God is with us.

An Exercise

As a couple, read 1 Corinthians 11:3-16 and Ephesians 5:21-33 (don't make the mistake of starting at verse 22!).

1. What is the context of each passage and the apparent concern of the writer?

2. What is the main teaching of each passage about the relationship of husband and wife?

3. Make a list of what the husband's headship is and is not, and what the wife's respect/submission is and is not *in your own marriage.*

4. In light of the above list discuss the following contemporary statements:

☐ A husband is responsible to make decisions on behalf of his wife.

☐ Men and women should function the same way in the marital relationship.

☐ Your role of husband or wife should be patterned after that played out by your parents.

☐ It is not healthy if your marriage roles resemble those of your parents.

☐ The husband is accountable to God for the wife's spirituality.

☐ The husband is over the wife, who is over the children, who is over the servants or pets in a chain-of-command.

☐ A wife will honor God by submitting to her husband's demands in a docile and compliant manner.

Part Three: Renovating

9
When the Marriage Is "For Worse"

TOM AND BEV WERE TWO OF THE "beautiful people." They had it made—a lovely home, upwardly mobile, young, healthy, with two bright children. They were both blessed with good looks and vivacious personalities. Their life was a full routine of work, ballet lessons for the children, racquetball and, as often as possible, expensive holidays. They had excellent relationships with their neighbors and good friends in the church. But they were hurting.

Though they enjoyed some good verbal communication—when they stopped long enough to talk—there was a tragic loneliness in their physical relationship. This loneliness was a deep surprise to both since they had passionately courted each other before getting married and never thought that "when" or "how often" or "whether to do it at all" could ever be issues in *their* marriage. Now they hardly ever dared talk about sex except to themselves: "Why is he so uninterested in me, when everyone else finds me so attractive?" "Why is she so sexually interested?"

Even a gentle initiative on Bev's part was misunderstood as a prelude to the demand for intercourse. She found it easier not to try than to be hurt once again. So they both buried themselves in their work. But they didn't bury the problem.

Bev had an affair. Their marriage had reached an all-time low. Each wanted a way out of a marriage that was now "for worse."

We must now explore the discipline of the covenant as it applies to two "for worse" marriages: (1) *the empty covenant*, where the marriage is one in legal status and public recognition, where there may even be the perfunctory submission to the marriage bed, but where there is no love; and (2) *the broken covenant*, where, like with Tom and Bev, for all practical purposes there is no longer a marriage and where, it is thought, divorce is the only reasonable and gracious solution.

I have refrained from dealing with the "stolen covenant"—cohabitation without covenant—because the remedy for this hurting almost-marriage is to enter fully into the covenant. Many people legally married, however, have the same kind of conditional, tentative arrangement and need just as much to enter into full covenant marriage.

The Empty Covenant

Loyal but loveless. It is particularly sad that some people believe they are honoring the Lord by enduring a loveless marriage. But God has something else in mind. And it is not divorce. Solving a loveless marriage by divorce would be like curing a disease by eliminating the patient.

A counselor and colleague of mine, Paddy Ducklow, tells me that divorce is not an event but a process. The separation of heart begins long before the physical separation. It often starts with the loss of little courtesies. Each divorcing person goes through a fairly typical progression of stages, some of them in a single day. Usually it takes somewhere between six months and two years to complete this well-documented emotional process:

Step 1: Disillusionment. The shroud of romantic fiction is shattered. People begin to question, "Is this all there is to love?" Then they start psychologically undressing the spouse, disqualifying the positive and catastrophizing the negative. Mentally they collect the negative to provide justification for marital erosion. It is also at this stage that the marital discord becomes a family matter. (Seventy-five per cent of divorces occur with children in the family.)

Step 2: Persistent Tension. Unresolved problems build and further strain the relationship. Couples start to compete with one another: "It's not that I want to win. It's that I need to beat you!" It is at this stage that they start avoiding one another, no longer confiding in or sharing with their spouse. If not already present, sexual problems crop up—for instance, frigidity and impotence, which reflect frozen anger. Put-downs, flirtations and bitter arguments are substituted for genuine intimacy and friendship.

Step 3: Detachment. This final stage is characterized by speechless animosity and mutual disrespect: "I just don't care anymore." Coldness becomes habitual. Boredom and apathy mask anger and vengeance, since it is easier to withdraw than to be wounded by attack. The couple also experiences a series of emotional deaths: death to their identities as good persons, spouses, caring parents; death to dreams and hopes of marriage; death to the fiction of who they imagined their spouse to be; death to their belief in healing, change and hope. They switch their orientation from past to future in their dreams, fantasies and concrete figuring about someone (something) else. They see separation as a solution: "Let's try to be apart to see if we can patch it up." If the issues are not dealt with, divorce follows.[1]

The covenant is a demanding reality. In the psalm of Asaph we are called first to "make vows to the LORD your God." But the line continues, *"and fulfill them"* (Ps 76:11). In our wedding vows we promise "to love," not to feel love forever, but to love. It is a decision we must continually make about our marriage partner.

Do we have an obligation to bless our spouse? Yes! It is what we promised on our wedding day: to love and to cherish. It is implicit in the covenant. Spouses have an obligation to bless in every appropriate way—honoring, listening, caring, continuing to court, giving each other the gift of intercourse, friendship and fidelity.

A spouse who is sexually faithful (that is, doesn't have an affair) but who withholds affection within the marriage is a covenant breaker. If a husband demands sexual love but refuses his wife friendship, he is a covenant-breaker. If spouses continually dishonor their marital partner in public and private and are unwilling to be publicly "on their side," they are covenant-breakers! A forty-nine-year-old woman said, "I'm committed to stay in this wretched relationship until the day I die!" She prided herself on keeping the covenant by refraining from sexual unfaithfulness. In fact, however, she was breaking the covenant by insisting that it be empty.

The solution for the empty covenant is not divorce but renewal. It takes two people to make a covenant. It takes only one to keep it. And usually it only takes one person willing to make a move, whether or not the spouse follows, to begin a healing process. Tough covenant love confronts the spouse with what is wrong and asks for change, being ready to go the second or third mile even before there is movement on the other side.

Not that blessing can be legislated. The Jewish Mishnah tried that in the first century. It spelled out in infinite detail the obligations of a marriage partner to bless. Commenting on Exodus 21:10, that a man must not deprive his wife of her marital rights, the rabbis offered a meticulous description of the wife's rights:

> If a man vowed to have no intercourse with his wife, the School of Shammai say: (She may consent) for two weeks. And the School of Hillel say: For one week (only). Disciples (of the Sages) may continue absent for thirty days against the will (of their wives) while they occupy themselves in the study of the Law; and labourers for one week. The *duty of marriage* enjoined in the Law is: every day for them that are unoccupied; twice a week for labourers; once a week for ass-drivers; once every thirty days for camel drivers; and once every six months for sailors.[2]

How much simpler is the advice of Paul: "Do not deprive each other except by mutual consent" (1 Cor 7:5)! Is the empty covenant doomed? No! The nature of the covenant requires both parties to fill the covenant with love *(hesed)*, with faithfulness. They can court each other again. The covenant is renewable.

The Broken Covenant

What if the covenant is broken? Perhaps one partner has betrayed the relationship with an affair. Or perhaps the relationship is just dead. A contemporary journal describes the easiest way out:

> One can love and live with another who is so totally different that extensive accommodation is required by both partners. It is possible, but is it worth it? The time comes when it is not; and the arrival of this rational adult decision,

Drawing by Dedini; © 1984, The New Yorker Magazine, Inc.

"Leonard, I'd like very much to get in touch with you if it's humanly possible."

while it may be cause for sadness at what is lost, is also a victory for good common sense. . . . If you and your mate decide that you want to end it, there is only one sensible thing to do: separate as quickly, completely and kindly as possible.[3]

Even the Archbishop of Canterbury Robert Runcie, when the Church of England gave provisional approval for divorced individuals to be married in the church, said, "Fidelity to something which has gone is like asking someone who is an agnostic to be martyred for the faith."[4] It is a stunning comparison dangerously near the truth. But it begs the question of whether the covenant is gone. Is the covenant annulled, dissolved, annihilated, when it is broken?

David Atkinson in *To Have and to Hold* finds, as I do, the covenant to be the key biblical idea for understanding marriage. But he *uses* the covenant idea to justify his position on divorce. Speaking of marriage as a covenant rather than a sacrament, he sees it as breakable. "If marriage is understood in covenant terms, the dissolution of a marriage (though always outside God's will for marriage, and therefore sinful) is not thereby impossible. Covenants, although intended and entered into as committed and permanent undertakings, can be broken."[5]

Sure, covenants can be broken. "Like Adam they broke covenant" is God's heartbroken cry (Hos 6:7). But there was still something of the covenant left. God had provided for covenant breaking in the sacrificial system. Christ's new covenant provides for us through "the blood of the covenant, which is poured out for many for the forgiveness of sins" (Mt 26:28). Neither the Old nor the New Testament provides for annulling or dissolving the covenant, at least from God's side.

Suppose I am speeding on the highway. A policeman stops my car and, as he approaches, I roll down my window. He leans over and says, "You have broken the law!" I try to hide my guilt and superciliously announce, "Actually I did not break the law. The law is still there. I didn't touch it. It's unharmed. I didn't annul it, honest!" Then realizing that he is not impressed by my argument I conclude, "I think I have just hurt myself in *trying* to break it!" For the sake of clarity, I might add, "I did indeed break the law, but I did not annul it."

Time and again Israel broke covenant with God. But Israel *couldn't* destroy the covenant even though they stopped living the lifestyle of a covenant people and failed to bless God in undivided worship. They violated the relationship, but the covenant itself was indissoluble.

The Perpetuity of the Covenant

We noted earlier three stages in the experience of covenant: the relational foundation, the obligations and the blessings. The blessings are conditional on the obligations. What if Israel refuses to keep the obligation? Then instead of blessings there are the curses. But they are the curses *of the covenant* (Deut 28:15-68). The covenant itself is unconditional.

God says, "I have made a covenant with my chosen one, I have sworn to David my servant, 'I will establish your line forever and make your throne firm through all generations' " (Ps 89:3). But what if they do not keep the demands of the covenant?

> If his sons forsake my law
>> and do not follow my statutes,
> if they violate my decrees
>> and fail to keep my commands,
> I will punish their sin with the rod,
>> their iniquity with flogging;
> but *I will not take my love [hesed]* from him,
>> nor will I ever betray my faithfulness.
> *I will not violate my covenant*
>> or alter what my lips have uttered.
> Once for all, I have sworn by my holiness—
>> and I will not lie to David—
> that his line will continue forever. (Ps 89:30-36)

We can lose the blessings but not the covenant. The glory of God's unconditional care is also our great hope for covenant marriage. There may still be restoration. Even if they do not repent God says that he will not reject them (Lev 26:14-45). The prophet Ezekiel sees God raising the nation from the dead to keep the covenant (Ezek 37). God offers Israel a new heart to replace their hard, stony heart (36:26). While Jesus said that divorce is for hardness of heart (Mt 19:8), a soft heart is the perennial gift of God to those in covenant who will receive it. Walther Eichrodt called this "an eternal and unalterable relationship of grace."[6]

Two people can be joined together by God in such a way that man cannot put them asunder. Biblically we can conceive of a couple who were divorced but are still in covenant. Many such couples, when there has not been remarriage, have been able to renew their covenant and to be remarried again legally.[7]

Hosea forces us to consider that, even though a marriage may be in tatters, the covenant can be maintained. When only he was keeping the covenant, both he and Gomer were still *in* the covenant.

Thinking the Unthinkable

As Christians we need not live by society's standards. We should not settle for less than God wills for us. We have in the Holy Spirit resources of soul healing and profound forgiveness which should make divorce unthinkable. Forsyth said, "Between two people confessing Christ and serving Him in the Spirit, divorce is unthinkable, and neither Christ nor Paul contemplates it. . . . Christianity opens moral resources which enables men and women to overcome the difficulties and disillusions of married life."[8]

Divorce relates to the human institution of marriage rather than the irrevocable covenant which Jesus was thinking of when he said, "What God has joined together, let man not separate." Although Atkinson says that "to argue that divorce is impossible is neither biblically warranted nor pastorally realistic,"[9] it does not seem so to me. Jesus said that it is "easier for heaven and earth to disappear than for the least stroke of a pen to drop out of the Law." In the very next verse he says, "Anyone who divorces his wife and marries another woman commits adultery" (Lk 16:17-18).[10] Speaking of this, John Howard Yoder says it is both theological and psychological nonsense to talk about a marriage as having been ended by divorce. The relationship may be negative, distant, vengeful or cold, but it is not erased. It still exists. The two will never be as they were before marriage.[11]

What can dissolve a covenant? Certainly not the stress of incompatability. Not even adultery can annul the covenant. Adultery is a grievous violation of the covenant but scripturally it is grounds more for forgiveness than for divorce. Even the decision of the two partners is not sufficient to dissolve the covenant. God has taken them at their word "until death them do part" (Rom 7:3). God joins. Only God can dissolve the covenant. And he chooses not to, for our good.

Confronting Your Spouse

The awesome statement "til death us do part" is not an excuse for everything. If we cannot walk away from the covenant, then we must work through our tough problems. Within a covenant are three healing movements that can restore commitment and bring richness back in: confronting, forgiving and courting your spouse.

It is safe to confront within the covenant. In fact, covenant love *[besed]* positively demands discipline within the covenant. It is tough love. God in the book of Hosea speaks roughly to his beloved: "My anger burns against them" (8:5); "I hated them there" (9:15); and "Woe to them, because they have strayed from me!" (7:13). Commenting on this and similar verses, James Mays says, "His anger is not bitter hatred; it is the passion that will not surrender in spite of frustration and rejection."[12]

"What do you consider your biggest fault, and what are you going to do about it?"

There are marriage partners who withhold the physical intimacy that could be the regular renewal of the covenant vows, though made in the privacy of the marriage bed. Each covenant partner has a responsibility to care enough to confront, even in this most sensitive of all areas. Sometimes, out of love for her husband, a Christian woman will knowingly permit her husband to have a mistress. To let a spouse "have his cake and eat it too" is unthinkable covenant love. Both partners are violating the covenant.

Love sometimes grows cold, and two people live what Henry David Thoreau called "lives of quiet desperation." No longer communicating, no longer sharing common interests, no longer sharing secret joys and sorrows, no longer sharing their fondest dreams, and no longer sharing a common bed. They seem to be "terminally unmarried." Either a public statement of the private divorce or the will to persist until death finally parts them seem to be the only live options. But there is another, and those in a covenant will seek it and do it.

Tough covenant love confronts the spouse with what is wrong, asks for change and offers to go the second and third mile toward accomplishing that change. There is always a right and wrong time, a right and wrong way, to bring about a confrontation. It never works when one is angry. One effective way is for the confronting spouse to ask the other when and how the issue should be discussed. One man chose the vehicle of a letter:

To my ever-loving wife,

During the past year I have attempted to seduce you 365 times. I succeeded thirty-six times. This averages once every ten days. The following is a list of excuses made on the unsuccessful occasions:

☐ We will wake the children: 7
☐ It's too hot: 15
☐ It's too cold: 3
☐ Too tired: 19
☐ It's too late: 16
☐ It's too early: 9
☐ Pretending to sleep: 33
☐ Windows open, neighbors will hear: 3
☐ Your back ached: 16
☐ Toothache: 2
☐ Headache: 26
☐ Giggling fit: 2
☐ I've had too much: 4
☐ Not in the mood: 21
☐ The baby is crying: 18
☐ Watched late show: 7

☐ Watched early show: 5
☐ Mudpack on: 12
☐ Grease on face: 6
☐ Reading Sunday paper: 10
☐ You are too drunk: 9
☐ We have company in the next room: 7
☐ Your parents are staying with us: 5
☐ Is that all you ever think about? 105

Do you think you could improve our record this coming year?

Your ever-loving husband[13]

The secret of managing covenant stress is to turn a "for worse" into a "for better." Confrontation is part of this. David Mace remarks with considerable insight, "There is no aloneness more complete than the aloneness that engulfs us when we are surrounded by people we cannot trust to tell us the truth!"[14]

Look for a radical healing. Consider Hosea's story (in modern terms): The minister's wife runs off with another man. That would be scandal enough, but this proves to be the first of a series of escapades. She goes to the streets once again. But God calls Hosea to do the impossible: "Go, show your love to your wife again" (3:1). Hosea buys her back, presumably from the slave market, or paying the bride price to her other husband. He restores her to his home and his love.

In Hosea 2, before he restores her, we get a peek at their home life. "Rebuke your mother," Hosea says to his three children, "rebuke her, for she is not my wife, and I am not her husband" (2:2). At first this looks like a divorce statement. But what is gloriously apparent to the thoughtful interpreter is this: this husband is not preoccupied with his legal rights to separation or the punishment of his guilty wife. He wants her back.[15] To win her he must use reality therapy. He must address the state of their covenant.

This husband will rise above his own "rights" in the marriage to find a way to restore his bride. He could have given her a bill of divorce (Deut 24:1-4). He might have arranged for her execution as an adulteress. But he seeks reconciliation.

What strikes us in the book of Hosea about the divine husbanding of God is what Mays calls "the assault of his love as husband and father upon their unfaithfulness."[16] He builds walls around his people to "hedge them in" (2:6); he withdraws his presence from them (5:6); he lets them drink the dregs of their disobedience (2:9-13); he lets them experience what can only be called the curses of the covenant. But he does all this because he is determined to keep his word. "I will heal their waywardness and love them freely" (14:4).

Covenant jealousy is different from the petty jealousy that springs from insecurity and fear that our marriage partners will find someone more attractive. It is a jealousy that is born of holy love, out of a desire that our partner will be called, wooed and won to the best in our relationship. As Mays says again, "Yahweh's love for Israel . . . was both passionately jealous and passionately generous, a love that closed the door on her sin and opened the door for her return to her husband."[17]

Hosea got his holy jealousy from the heart of God. Would that we had the same heart! With it would come loving confrontation.

Forgiving Your Spouse
The heart of covenant renewal is forgiveness. The story of Hosea makes that clear. The entire sacrificial system was God's provision for people who had broken the covenant unintentionally. For willful sin there was only the sheer mercy of God, which is not lacking.

Forgiveness is a costly matter. The death and resurrection of Jesus are the ultimate provision of God for covenant forgiveness and renewal. In marriage the *only* breach that cannot be healed is the permanent stepping out of the covenant by both parties. Forgiveness is the solvent of broken relationships within the covenant.

It is said that the hardest words to utter are "I'm sorry." Harder still are the words "I forgive you." Sometimes we are schizophrenic, our heads Christian but our hearts pagan. We "think" forgiveness but don't live it. We know God has forgiven us a million-dollar debt, and yet we hold a five-dollar debt against our spouse. God has heard us say in the Lord's prayer that we want him to forgive us just as much as we forgive everyone else. No wonder Augustine called it a terrible prayer! We read in Scripture that God *cannot* forgive us unless we forgive those who have hurt us (Mt 18:35). Why then do we not forgive?

One reason is that we forget how much we have been forgiven. That fact alone ought to inspire an uncalculating forgiveness. Another reason is our own pharisaism when we thank God that we are not like others (Lk 18:9-14), or—worse still— that we *are* like others. Sometimes we would rather see our marriage grind into deadness, out of a terrible pride, than release a flood of healing by humbling ourselves before our spouse and admitting that we could be wrong.

Sometimes we don't forgive because we think we cannot until our spouse repents. It is true that our spouse will not feel forgiven until there is repentance, but forgiveness (in the giving) is not dependent on repentance. Our kindness might in time lead our spouse to repentance, as God's kindness does (Rom 2:4). It is an environment that makes repentance easy.

But sometimes we don't forgive (or do not feel forgiven) because we don't now *how.* I have learned these things about forgiveness: (1) it must be specific; (2) it must be verbalized; (3) it must be heartfelt; and (4) it must be maintained.

We must be specific because general forgiveness means little. If we have been hurt, we need to verbalize our forgiveness quickly, before the sun goes down (Eph 4:26). We must not do it to lay guilt, but to release the relationship from the paralysis that unforgiven sin brings.

When we are the offender, we must make the first move as well. I find it unthinkable Christianly to take the position Atkinson does, that unless the sin has "come into the open" we need not confess it.[18] In a marriage, silence is violence and secret sins are Satanic.

Forgiveness must be from the heart because it is a *decision*. It is an act of will, not a feeling. Therefore it is important actually to say, "I forgive you." It is not good enough to say something general like, "I guess I'm no saint either." We need to say (or to hear) the words "I forgive you."

The words having been spoken, forgiveness needs to be maintained. We must discipline our thoughts when we relapse even briefly into resentment or self-condemnation. God's amazing grace means that our past is in the past. We can offer no less to our spouses if we have been touched at all by God's forgiveness.

An old form of the Lord's Prayer contains a suggestive phrase: "forgive us our debts as we forgive our debtors." When a debt is forgiven, it means there is no further obligation for the transaction. The creditor does not say, "I will offer you an easier repayment schedule," or "I will waive interest payments for the first twelve months." He says, "You are completely forgiven. You are without further obligation to me." Forgiveness is not *for* anything at all except the restoration of an unconditional relationship of belonging. That is how God forgives us and how we must forgive one another.

If we find ourselves unable to forgive from the heart, it may be an invitation from God to do a deeper work in us. Through

Gail's inner-healing ministry (or prayer counseling, as it is sometimes called) we find that some people are able to allow Jesus to take them back *with him* to those painful experiences in their youth and childhood that affect their capacity to give and receive forgiveness.[19]

But forgiveness alone is not enough to heal the covenant. Courting is needed, the renewal of the love relationship itself.

Courting Your Spouse

Courting is more important after marriage than before. It is apparently a lost art. According to the Oxford dictionary, *court* is a transitive verb that means "to make love to; to entice; to seek to win." The derivative word *courtesan* refers to a prostitute! The ancient Greek Demosthenes once said that his society had courtesans for the sake of pleasure, concubines for daily cohabitation and wives for having children and doing housework. Courtship hardly seems a worthy subject for Christian marriage!

But courting is exactly what is needed in an empty or a broken covenant. We must continue to "find" our partner, to open doors of response (the word *allure* means to create an opening), to win our rightful place in our spouse's life.

Therefore I am now going to allure her;
I will lead her into the desert
and speak tenderly to her. (Hos 2:14)

Covenant love makes our God and his prophet on earth do something radical, something crazy. It is as beautiful as the alabaster jar poured over the head of Jesus, gloriously wasteful, when these two despised husbands set out to court their wives.

We have to imagine Hosea walking down Main Street Samaria and seeing in the city square, where the slaves were being auctioned off, his own wife. She had degenerated from being a minister's wife to a mistress, from being a mistress to a prostitute, from being a prostitute to a slave. She could not go further down. But at the bottom of the pit was covenant love!

Something in Hosea's heart said, she is mine. And he bought her for half the price of a slave. Then he restored her to his home, and forbade her to go with any other man. It seems that, although it was his right, he abstained from physical intimacy with her for a period of time (3:3). He waited until she wanted him to come to her. That is courting within the covenant.

In hindsight Tom and Bev might have said with Hosea, "I take you for worse." But by God's grace their "for worse" marriage became a "for better" one. It took all three healing movements: confronting, forgiving and courting.

Bev risked all to tell Tom about her affair. It was painful to do so but not as painful as the burden of guilt that hung over her like a dark depressing cloud. Forgiveness does not come easily or quickly when the wound runs so deep.

"I'm no Hosea," Tom said to his confidant. But it turned out that he was. Tom did forgive Bev and welcomed Bev into his heart in a new way. But Tom had some confessing to do too.

While they were courting before marriage Tom had been unfaithful to Bev. He carried the guilt of this into his marriage, partly because he had never told Bev. Though he had asked God's forgiveness many times he did not *feel* forgiven and he had never forgiven himself. Bev, too, was invited to have the heart of Hosea and to come to the place of saying, "I forgive you," which is the same as saying, "I will treat you as though you had not sinned against me."

It is a gracious God that takes our "for worse" experiences and makes them "for better." Tom and Bev, doubly forgiven and doubly loved by God and each other, set out to court each other again. There were still problems and growing pains in their relationship, but by building on the indissoluble covenant they made "the Valley of Achor [trouble] a door of hope"

(Hos 2:15). They became not only happy, but content, as God continued to renew their covenant.

An Exercise

The tender courting passage in Hosea 2:14-19 gives us some important clues for the process of renewing our love relationship in a marriage. After each point I will suggest a question that can be answered by a spouse to help the courting process.

1. Courting is a *winning* appeal. It is positive persuasion, creating an opening for yourself. But the true lover will never do anything to suspend the other's judgment or to restrict the other's freedom through manipulation. The lover is infatuated but does not overwhelm the loved one.

Ask your spouse, or future spouse, to complete this sentence: What you need to know about my feelings right now is . . .

2. Courting is a *warm* appeal. The Hebrew phrase for wooing is literally a translation of three Hebrew words meaning "speak to the heart." Courting love is not addressed first to the intellect but to the heart, by the sheer strength and vulnerability of love laid on the heart from a heart.

Complete this sentence for your spouse or future spouse: You can express warmth to me by . . .

3. Courting is a *wise* appeal. The biblical heart is not all goo, sheer unfocused emotion. The heart is the totality of a person's inner life: emotion, mind and will. It includes moral judgment and what we Christians call conscience. More is demanded of the courtier than the courtesan, as Hosea's list of betrothal qualities in 2:19 suggests: righteousness, justice, love *[hesed]*, compassion, faithfulness. It is these qualities which we should both give and call forth in courting.

Complete this sentence to share with the loved one: What we need to talk about for you to know me better is . . .

4. Courting is a *waiting* appeal. Respect for the person calls us to wait until response can be freely given. Love can never be forced either in the giving or in the receiving.

Gail wanted to "find" me and court me one anniversary. So she handprinted a love poem in calligraphy:

When you came, you were like
   red wine and honey,
And the taste of you burnt
   my mouth with its sweetness.

Now you are like morning bread,
   I hardly taste you at all
   for I know your savor,
But I am completely nourished.
I felt well courted. And I treasure the remembrance of it.

10
Married for Good

WHAT IS COVENANT MARRIAGE? It is sharing a secret with someone who is yours. It is a quiet but knowing look across the room. It is daring to speak the unspeakable for the sake of your relationship. It is risking your most personal self because there is a net beneath. It is accepting and forgiving. It is laughter in the night. It is coming home after an impossible day to meet someone who has also had an impossible day, and collapsing together on the sofa. It is the joy of belonging unconditionally.

Oh, the comfort,
the inexpressible joy
of feeling at home with a person,
having neither to measure words

nor mince phrases,
knowing that the other
will gently sift the wheat,
and with the breath of kindness
blow the chaff away.[1]

Double Marriage

Covenant marriage is our Maker's design for our living, and a great gift. Greater still is to know acceptance with the Maker himself through a personal covenant with Jesus. But the greatest joy is reserved for two people who belong *together*, unconditionally, to Christ. Because of Christ's death and resurrection we sinners can belong to a holy God. Christ proposes marriage to us, an irrevocable covenant with all the blessings and obligations implicit in that new covenant. We have only to say the nuptial yes—yes to our earthly spouse, and yes to our heavenly groom. What a delightful double marriage! "A cord of three strands is not quickly broken" (Eccles 4:12).

It was not a dreamy, modern sentimentalist but a second-century saint in the toughest of times who wrote some of the most exalted words about the double covenant of two Christians in marriage. I can offer no higher ideal for our own generation, nor any more hopeful invitation than these words of Tertullian (ca. A.D. 160-225):

How shall we ever be able adequately to describe the happiness of that marriage which the Church arranges, the Sacrifice strengthens, upon which the blessing sets a seal, at which angels are present as witnesses, and to which the Father gives his consent? For not even on earth do children marry properly and legally without their father's permission.

How beautiful, then, the marriage of two Christians, two who are one in hope, one in desire, one in the way of life they follow, one in the religion they practice. They are as brother and sister, both servants of the same Master. Nothing divides them, either in flesh or in spirit. They are, in very truth, "two in one flesh"; and where there is but one flesh there so also but one spirit. They pray together, they worship together, they fast together; instructing one another, encouraging one another, strengthening one another. Side by side they visit God's church and partake of God's Banquet; side by side they face difficulties and persecution, share their consolations. . . . They need not be furtive about making the Sign of the Cross, nor timorous in greeting the brethren, nor silent in asking a blessing of God.[2]

Here is no mere youthful idealism. This ideal is too precious to be lost in the process of aging. It comes from the plan and purpose of our covenant-making God. He is determined to stamp his image on earth and to do that especially in family, marriage and home. If this covenant ideal were to die, then something within us would not be worth living. We would not even know that we had exchanged a shadow for the glory of the real thing.

A Firm Foundation

It is a decade now since I built that first unit on our island cabin. Now we have three units delightfully integrated with the environment, all sitting on a good, firm foundation. I hardly ever think about the foundation now, but I know it's there and I inspect it from time to time. Everything else depends on it.

Cantilevered over the water, a small deck is secured to the main supports under the building. It is a good place to talk. Sitting there, we feel as comfortable as we do in a well-weathered and secure relationship.

Gail and I and my brother's in-laws were there one Saturday afternoon in the fall, enjoying the flaming red berries on the arbutus trees that make our coastal autumns at least a good

second to the inland spectacle. Albert Swim, my brother's fa-
ther-in-law, and his wife, Carrie, had just celebrated their fif-
tieth anniversary. Albert used to be the foreman of a mill at a
Nova Scotia seaport, where they lived all their lives. His ruddy
face, etched and lined and with a permanent maritime blush,
is worthy of portraiture. It reveals the peace and the love that
have marked those fifty years together.

I like to think that in some appreciable way their faces have
been slightly transfigured by the love they have for each other
and for God. They have zest for life together in all of its fullness
that has not waned as the years passed. With a twinkle in their
eyes they do not hesitate to tell you how important their physical affection has been to them over the years. They are still
enviably in love. They know the riches of covenant.

Sitting with them over the expanse of water, I could not let
the moment pass.

"What do you think is the secret of your marriage?" I asked.
They seemed unprepared for the question, so I followed up
with some suggestions. "Did you have any premarital counseling before you got married?"

"No."

"Have you ever gone to a marriage counselor?"

"No, not that either," Carrie said.

"Have you ever gone to one of these marriage enrichment
weekends such as Gail and I conduct out here?"

"No."

"Have you read some good books about marriage?" (I had
an ulterior motive for that one.)

"Can't say that we have!"

Now I was really fishing. I might not have this opportunity
again. Why are some people so well married? I asked one final
question: "Have you ever given a lot of thought about how to
get married for good?"

"No."

"*That*," I suggested, as we all broke into gales of laughter, "*that* has to be the secret!"

But it isn't, not today at least. Today we have to think about it. Frankly I suspect Albert and Carrie have thought about it more than they realize. In Albert and Carrie's day, when they said their vows they meant them—*forever*.

It can be that way for us too. We can ponder those covenant vows one by one *before* we say them. We can mean them *when* we say them. And, for some of us, *long after* is not too late to begin to mean them.

An Exercise

This is a meditation for married people and may be used by a couple as a guided meditative prayer.

1. *God made us.* "For you created my inmost being; you knit me together in my mother's womb" (Ps 139:13). Thank God that he created you and your spouse to be the unique persons you are in physical stature, emotional capacity, personality and spiritual potential.

2. *God made us in his image* (Gen 1:26-27). Thank God that he made you to be a creative expression of himself. Humbly welcome the privilege, honor and responsibility of imaging God.

3. *God made us male and female* (Gen 1:27). Thank him for the differences. Think of the qualities in your spouse that you identify as those of the opposite sex. Welcome and celebrate these qualities as good gifts of God.

4. *God made us from each other and for each other* (Gen 2:22). The woman was taken out of the man and the man found himself again in the woman. Thank God that the woman was not made to be an assistant man but to be a helper as his opposite and he to her.

5. *The Lord God brought the woman to the man* (Gen 2:22). How did you find each other? What brought you together? Thank God that he was involved in bringing you to each other. Believe that he is still actively bringing you together for companionship and for his glory. Welcome his sovereignty and transforming purpose that makes his call and his plan more significant than your decisions.

6. *The man and his wife were both naked and were not ashamed* (Gen

2:25). Thank God for the capacity he has given you to say "I love you" with your body, soul and spirit. Thank him for those times when there has been nothing between you, when communication has been open, when nothing needed to be hidden.

7. *The man and his wife knew they were naked . . . and made coverings for themselves* (Gen 3:7). Recognize what sin does to your intimacy and how futile it is to cover yourself with self-justification, a pretense of strength or weakness, roles or masks.

8. *The Lord God made garments of skin for Adam and his wife and clothed them* (Gen 3:21). Thank God that you can risk being completely honest with all that is inside you because Christ covers you. God has made a covering. By faith envisage Christ putting a robe of righteousness over you, the result of his shed blood and finished work on the cross. Let him wrap it around you until you are completely secure, secure enough to reveal yourself just as you are to your spouse. Thank him.

9. *God said: Go show your love to your spouse again* (Hos 3:1). If some coldness has set in, if the little kindnesses have long vanished, if you are beginning to think that someone else may be more understanding, hear this word! God says, "Show your love again." Invite God to help you to find your spouse emotionally again and to show love.

10. *Wives submit to your husbands as to the Lord. . . . Husbands love your wives as Christ loved the church. . . . Submit to one another out of reverence for Christ* (Eph 5:22, 25, 21). Thank God that your relationship is a sacramental means of expressing the relationship of Jesus with his people. Pray that in mutual submission you may increasingly find a way of being husband or wife to God's glory.

11. *What God has joined together let man not separate* (Mt 19:6). Will you forever renounce the thought of seeking a way out of the relationship? Rest, even rejoice, that you are committed until death parts you. Worship God who dwells in covenant and shares in covenant-making with us and is determined to strengthen it.

12. *Though one may be overpowered, two can defend themselves. A cord of three strands is not quickly broken* (Eccles 4:12). Consciously welcome the "third strand" in your marriage—the living Christ. Give him permission to be interwoven with you. Let his strength and love bind you together.

13. *God is love and he who dwells in love dwells in God* (1 Jn 4:16). Thank him that you can be anywhere with anyone and experience the highest joy of a human being: to dwell in God and to be indwelt by God.

Notes

Chapter 1: First Things First

[1]P. T. Forsyth, *Marriage: Its Ethic and Religion* (London: Hodder and Stoughton, n.d.), p. 120.

[2]David Atkinson, *To Have and to Hold: The Marriage Covenant and the Discipline of Divorce* (Grand Rapids, Mich.: Eerdmans, 1979), p. 70.

[3]Gestalt prayer, quoted in E. A. Griffin, *The Mind Changers* (Wheaton, Ill.: Tyndale, 1983), p. 32.

[4]R. D. Laing, *The Politics of the Family* (Toronto: CBC Publications, 1969), p. 2.

[5]Ibid., pp. 1-2.

[6]Dietrich Bonhoeffer, *Letters and Papers from Prison* (London: SCM Books, 1953), p. 69.

[7]It is remarkable that Margaret Mead, who is infamous for her proposal of a five-year renewable marriage contract, was also quoted in a university lecture as saying that the most dangerous thing happening in the United States today is that people are entering marriage with the idea that it could be terminated.

[8]Forsyth, *Marriage*, p. 114.

Chapter 2: God's Covenant Design

[1]Lewis Smedes, *Mere Morality* (Grand Rapids, Mich.: Eerdmans, 1983), p. 161.

[2]The most comprehensive treatment of this subject is Walther Eichrodt, *Theology of the Old Testament*, vol. 1, trans. J. A. Baker (Philadelphia: Westminster Press, 1961). Eichrodt sees the covenant as the rubric for interpreting and understanding the message of the Old Testament.

[3]R. K. Harrison, *Introduction to the Old Testament* (Grand Rapids, Mich: Eerdmans, 1975), p. 582.

[4]Chaim Potok, *Wanderings: Chaim Potok's History of the Jews* (New York: Fawcett Crest, 1978), p. 111.

[5]The basic form of the agreements made between monarchs and their vassals (suzerainty treaties) in the Hittite empires, second millennium B.C., followed a familiar pattern: "a *preamble* or title, which identified the instigator of the covenant; a *historical prologue,* which reviewed past relations between the suzerain and the vassal and indicated that past benefactions by the former constituted grounds for gratitude and future obedience on the part of the latter; *basic and detailed stipulations,* imposed by the great king upon the vassal; a provision for the *deposition and public reading* of the covenant at intervals by the vassal; a list of *deities as witnesses* to the agreement; and an enumeration of the *blessings or curses* consequent upon either observance or neglect of the covenant provisions" (R. K. Harrison, *Jeremiah and Lamentations: An Introduction and Commentary* [Downers Grove, Ill.: InterVarsity Press, 1973], p. 25). The parallel with God's covenant with Israel is understandable. However, the emphasis of the Israelite covenant is more on the preamble and historical prologue than on the stipulations, on *being* more than *doing,* on grace and gratitude more than obligation and obedience.

[6]Elmer Smick, "Berith-Covenant," in Harris, Archer, and Waltke, eds. *Theological Wordbook of the Old Testament,* vol. 1 (Chicago: Moody Press, 1980), p. 129.

[7]Karl Barth, paraphrased in Atkinson, *To Have and to Hold,* p. 70.

[8]Dunstan, as quoted in ibid., pp. 75-76.

[9]G. R. Dunstan, *Theology* 78, no. 659 (May 1975):245-49.

Chapter 3: Saying "I Do"

[1]Quoted in Kirk Farnsworth, "The Myth of the Machine" in Stephen Board, ed., *HIS Guide to Sex, Singleness and Marriage* (Downers Grove, Ill.: InterVarsity Press, 1977), p. 48.

[2]Lance Morrow, "The Hazards of Homemade Vows," *Time,* 27 June 1983, p. 78.

[3]*The Alternative Service Book 1980: Services Authorized for Use in the Church of England in Conjunction with The Book of Common Prayer* (Cambridge: SPCK, 1980), p. 290. A fascinating study of the history of Christian marriage rites was written by Kenneth Stevenson, *Nuptial Blessing* (New York: Oxford University Press, 1983).

[4]Martin Buber, *I and Thou,* trans. Ronald Gregor Smith (Edinburgh: T & T Clark, 1958).

[5]Ibid., p. 3.

[6]Ibid., p. 8.

[7]Shailer Mathews, "Marriage," in James Hastings, ed., *A Dictionary of Christ*

and the Gospels, 2 vols. (Edinburgh: T & T Clark, 1913), 2:136-38.

[8]I only partly agree with C. S. Lewis when he calls for a sharp distinction between marriage governed by the state and marriage governed by the church. See C. S. Lewis, *Mere Christianity* (London: Geoffrey Bles, 1953), pp. 88-89.

[9]Quoted in Maureen Baker, ed., *The Family: Changing Trends in Canada* (Toronto: McGraw Hill Ryerson, 1984), p. 90.

[10]Walter R. Schrumm, "Sex Should Occur Only within Marriage," in *Current Issues in Human Sexuality,* ed. Harold Feldman and Andrea Parrot Eggleston (Beverly Hills, Calif.: Sage Publications, 1984), p. 9.

[11]Hans Watree Wolff, *Anthropology of the Old Testament,* trans. Margaret Kohl (Philadelphia: Fortress Press, 1974), pp. 74-80.

[12]Smedes, *Mere Morality,* pp. 16-19.

Chapter 4: Six Loves

[1]Taken from Joseph Stein, *The Fiddler on the Roof* (New York: Crown, 1964).

[2]It is now generally agreed, for example, that the interchanging of *philia* and *agape* in John 21:15-17 is for stylistic reasons rather than a change of meanings.

[3]W. Gunther and H. G. Link, "Agape," in Colin Brown, ed., *The New International Dictionary of New Testament Theology,* 3 vols. (Grand Rapids, Mich.: Zondervan, 1971), 2:542.

[4]Chaim Potok, *The Chosen* (Greenwich: Faucett Crest Book, 1967), p. 74.

[5]Ailred of Rievaulx, *Spiritual Friendship,* trans. Eugenia Laker (Kalamazoo, Mich.: Cistercian Publications, 1977), pp. 53-54. Ailred develops friendship in terms of loyalty, a concept we will explore later in *hesed.*

[6]There is at least one other Hebrew word that I do not develop in this chapter, the word *dod,* which, when used in the Song of Songs comes close to the Greek word *eros.*

[7]Wolff, *Anthropology of the Old Testament,* pp. 174-75.

[8]John White, *Eros Defiled: The Christian and Sexual Sin* (Downers Grove, Ill.: InterVarsity Press, 1977), pp. 18-19.

[9]Other passages using *racham* this way are 2 Chron 30:9; Ps 51:1; 103:4; Is 13:18; Jer 21:7.

[10]Eliczek 32. Quoted in Benjamin Schlesinger and Shirley Tenhuse Giblon, "Lasting Marriages" (Guidance Centre, Faculty of Education, University of Toronto, Ontario, 1984), p. vii.

[11]Told in F. W. Boreham, *The Prodigal* (London: Epworth Press, n.d.), p. 15.

[12]Norman Snaith, *The Distinctive Ideas of the Old Testament* (New York: Schocken Books, 1969), p. 131.

[13]Examples of how *ahaba* is used for the love between a man and woman are Gen 29:20; 2 Sam 1:26; Prov 5:19; Eccles 9:6; Song 5:8; 8:6.

[14]That is behind the extraordinary allegory of Ezekiel 16:4-60. The Old Testament uses *ababa* thirty-two times for God's love.

[15]James H. Olthuis. *I Pledge You My Troth: A Christian View of Marriage, Family and Friendship* (New York: Harper and Row, 1975), p. 21.

[16]Ibid., p. 20; emphasis mine.

[17]Ibid., p. 26.

[18]Other uses of *hesed* in the Old Testament are Ps 17:7; 25:6; 40:11; Is 63:7; Jer 9:24; 31:3; 32:18; Hos 2:19.

Chapter 5: Six Loyalties

[1]Smedes, *Mere Morality,* p. 161.

[2]Ibid., p. 169.

[3]Ibid., p. 170.

[4]Quoted in Roy Fairchild, *Christians in Families* (Richmond, Va.: Covenant Life Curriculum, 1964), p. 65.

Chapter 6: The Ten Commandments of Marriage

[1]Gordon Wenham, "Grace and Law in the Old Testament," in Bruce Kaye and Gordon Wenham, eds., *Law, Morality and the Bible* (Downers Grove, Ill.: InterVarsity Press, 1978), p. 17.

[2]Eichrodt, *Theology of the Old Testament,* 1:92, 250.

Chapter 7: Sexuality and the Mystery of Unity

[1]Alan Ecclestone in *Yes to God,* quoted in Robert Wild, *Frontiers of the Spirit: A Christian View of Spirituality* (Toronto: Anglican Book Centre, 1981), p. 23.

[2]Richard Rohr, "An Appetite for Wholeness," in *Sojourners* (November 1982), p. 30.

[3]Bil Gilbert, "You Could Be Better Than You Are . . ." in *Time,* 18 June 1984.

[4]Dolores Leckey, *A Family Spirituality* (New York: Crossroad, 1982), p. 17.

[5]Smedes, *Mere Morality,* p. 180.

[6]Vancouver Symphony Orchestra "Programme Notes," 13 March 1983.

[7]Søren Kierkegaard, *Sickness unto Death* (Garden City, N.Y.: Doubleday, 1954), p. 183.

[8]Some of these thoughts are carefully developed in Helmut Thielicke, "Mystery of Sexuality," in *Are You Nobody?* (Richmond: John Knox Press, 1965), pp. 45-60.

[9]Forsyth, *Marriage,* p. 33.

[10]Aquinas *Summa Theologica* 11. 154. art. 11. ad. 3.

[11]Smedes, *Mere Morality,* p. 168.

[12]*Time,* 27 December 1982, p. 57.

[13]Lewis B. Smedes, *Sex for Christians* (Grand Rapids, Mich.: Eerdmans, 1976),

p. 34.

Chapter 8: The Problem of Headship

[1]Aileen Kraitor, ed., *Up from the Pedestal* (Chicago, 1968).

[2]*The Alternative Service Book 1980*, p. 291.

[3]Alan Stibbs, *The First Epistle General of Peter* (Grand Rapids, Mich.: Eerdmans, 1979), p. 125; emphasis mine.

[4]Wendy Dennis, "To Be or Not to Be," in *Homemakers Magazine* (September 1984), p. 44.

[5]See, for example, Larry Christenson, *The Christian Family* (Minneapolis: Bethany Fellowship, 1970), p. 17. Basic Youth Conflicts (Bill Gothard) has proposed the chain-of-command, though he has somewhat modified his teaching on this.

[6]*"Neged"* in Brown, Driver and Briggs, *A Hebrew and English Lexicon of the Old Testament* (London: Oxford University Press, 1959), p. 617.

[7]*"Kephalē,"* in Bauer, *A Greek—English Lexicon of the New Testament*, trans. William F. Arndt and F. Wilbur Gingrich (Chicago: University of Chicago Press, 1959), p. 431.

[8]Berkley and Alvera Mickelson, "The 'Head' of the Epistles," *Christianity Today* (February 20, 1981), pp. 20-23.

[9]James Hurley, *Man and Woman in Biblical Perspective* (Grand Rapids, Mich.: Zondervan, 1981), p. 166.

[10]Ibid., p. 176.

[11]Hurley makes this unfortunate error in *Man and Woman*, p. 146.

[12]"Christ is the head of the man" is taken by James Hurley to mean that Christ takes the place of the last Adam, as head of mankind (ibid., p. 167). But the simplest understanding of this short statement is to see it as one more statement of priority within an interdependent relationship.

[13]Patricia Gundry, *Heirs Together* (Grand Rapids, Mich.: Zondervan, 1980), p. 137.

[14]See Hurley, *Man and Woman*, p. 207.

[15]Ibid., p. 151.

Chapter 9: When the Marriage Is "For Worse"

[1]Adapted from Sheila Kessler, *The American Way of Divorce* (Chicago: Nelson-Hall, 1975).

[2]Nashim 5.6 in Herbert Danby, *The Mishnah* (Oxford: University Press, 1977), p. 252.

[3]Stephen Johnson, "If You Can't Envision Your Future—Without Your Lost Love," in *New Woman*, September/October 1979, p. 73.

[4]Quoted in "One More Try," in *Time*, 23 July 1984, p. 59.

[5]Atkinson, *To Have and to Hold*, p. 135.

[6]Eichrodt, *Theology of the Old Testament*, p. 467.

[7]Scripture forbids the return of a spouse to his or her first marital partner

if they have remarried. The divorce legislation in Deut 24:1-4 had this situation in view.

[8]Forsyth, *Marriage*, p. 22, 39.

[9]Atkinson, *To Have and to Hold*, p. 152.

[10]I am well aware of the so-called exception clauses found in Matthew 5 and 19. A full treatment of the divorce passages would require a book in itself. But I believe the evangelical consensus that permits divorce for adultery or desertion must be biblically challenged. Dr. Peter Davids, conducting an exegetical study for *The Equippers* on "Divorce and the Church" made some crucial remarks in a yet-unpublished paper ("Divorce: The Biblical Data," *The Equippers*, Vancouver, 1985, pp. 5-7). I quote here a portion:

Some further points should be noted while on this set of texts. First, Matthew, unlike Mark and Luke, presents only the man as divorcing or committing adultery by remarrying, which is in accordance with Jewish legal practice. The other gospels present the teaching as reciprocal to a degree in accordance with Roman law.

Second, Matthew's well-known exception clause ("except in the case of unchastity") must also apply to a point of Jewish law. Two possibilities present themselves: (a) that if the woman has been unfaithful one cannot *make* her commit adultery, for she has already done so of her own accord. This fits Matt. 5:32 well and the complete form may be assumed in the more cryptic Matt. 19:9. The real problem is that the Greek *porneia* is a rather unusual term for adultery (the normal Greek term is *moicheia*). Or (b) that he is excepting the possibility, important in Jewish law, that the woman had had pre-marital intercourse of which he was not informed until after marriage. While in the Old Testament such cases of marriage under false pretenses could have resulted in execution, divorce would have been more likely in the New Testament period (cf. Joseph in Matt. 1). This allows Jesus to notice one subtlety of Jewish law, yet does not weaken his statement.

Third, Jesus' point resolves on the argument that one cannot really divorce. Since God made the union, humans cannot dissolve it. Thus the divorce decree is a legal fiction. The parties involved (including the judge in our society) have sinned, but they have not ended the marriage. Only on such an assumption can one say that remarriage or marrying a properly divorced woman is adultery. And that is precisely what Jesus does say. As John Howard Yoder has pointed out, it is both theological and psychological nonsense to talk about a marriage as having been ended by divorce. The relationship may be negative, distant, revengeful, or cold, but it is not erased. It still exists. The two will never be as they were before marriage.

Finally, note that since Jesus rejected Deuteronomy as a permission for divorce, it is never referred to by Paul. It ceases to have relevance except in the case of a woman or man desiring to return to a former spouse after a re-marriage to a second spouse has terminated. Even there its relevance may be limited by the New Testament's knowledge of the forgiveness of sin in a way mostly unknown in the Old Testament.

[11]Videotaped course on ethics at Regent College, Vancouver.

[12]James Luther Mays, *Hosea: A Commentary* (Philadelphia: Westminster Press, 1969), p. 119.

[13]Jack Dominian, *Marital Breakdown* (Chicago: Franciscan Herald Press, 1968), pp. 79-80.

[14]Quoted in Dorothy T. Samuel, *Fun and Games in Marriage* (Waco, Tex.: Word Books, 1973), pp. 88-89.

[15]Mays, *Hosea,* p. 38.

[16]Ibid., p. 14.

[17]Ibid., p. 58.

[18]Atkinson, *To Have and to Hold,* p. 136. I could only hope, as Gordon Wenham does in commenting on this, that he slipped his pen at this point. I have heard it forcibly argued, however, that a step toward healing old sins and hurts is to confess first to a minister, priest or trusted Christian friend. This would prevent clouding the immediate initiative in marital healing. By focusing on present communication and by avoiding garbage dumping, healing is facilitated. Eventually walking in the light requires a full confession to one's spouse.

[19]A helpful book on inner healing is Rita Bennett, *How to Pray for Inner Healing for Yourself and Others* (Old Tappan, N.J.: Fleming H. Revell, 1984).

Chapter 10: Married for Good

[1]A poem ascribed to George Eliot.

[2]"Ad Uxorem," quoted in Kenneth Stevenson, *Nuptial Blessing: A Study in Christian Marriage Rites* (New York: Oxford University Press, 1983), p. 17.

CPSIA information can be obtained
at www.ICGtesting.com
Printed in the USA
BVHW071339200319
543197BV00003B/398/P

9 781573 830874